DEDICATION

Lynn, my wife, you are the sun in my life, shining through the clouds even on those stormy days, filling my world with your love and beauty. You've always supported me, even when you thought better. You've helped me grow and become who I am today.

My children, I am so very grateful and honored for being your father. I can see a part of myself in each one of you. You are all very beautiful souls, and your hearts are so warm and kind. You have taught me so much about myself. Thank you for your love and understanding.

Mother, I'm grateful to you for being you and for overcoming seemingly insurmountable odds in your life. For taking care of me when I was sickly as a child. Due to our relationship, I was able to become the man I am today and gain the ability to teach so many other people many things to improve the quality of their lives. I also learned from you forgiveness and the importance of not just following the crowd, but questioning things.

Dad, thank you for your understanding and for doing your best in raising me. I didn't see it much, but when I did, your childlike heart was so kind, fun, and encouraging.

Grandpa, thank you for letting me spend so much time on your yacht. You have no idea what that meant to me. Thank you for just being you.

Stepmom Shirley, thank you for doing what you could with me when you had your chance, even though I was a handful at the time.

Me (why not?), thank you for overcoming all you did in your life so that you could share your story. It was a long time coming, but you did it. Yay!

Carol, you have been the driving force throughout my life to keep me moving forward. You kept me alive so many times so that I could accomplish what I was sent here to do.

Bob, thank you for your friendship, for being a good friend, someone who was always there if I wanted a hand.

Joy, I love your authenticity, which is what makes you so great. Thank you, "big sister," for your love, understanding, and kindness. Thank you from the depth of the heart of my soul for sharing your universal knowledge and thoughts, which allowed me to reach new levels in awareness and empowered me to realize my own divinity within. Thank you for your love for me and your love for all of humanity.

Anna, you look past my words and journey into the spirit of my heart for the meaning. You saw something within me that was buried, and you unearthed it with your love and compassion. It is the essence of who I truly am. In the process, I also discovered the essence of who you truly are. Your thoughts and intentions have had an impact on my life and this book. You, my friend, are a remarkable woman and a beautiful soul.

Reader, thank you for your interest in my book. You were my motivation to write about my life. My intention from the first word I wrote in these pages was that it would have a positive impact on your life or the life of someone you know and, in some small way, make your life better.

CONTENTS

PROLOGUE

This is the story of my journey through the valley of the shadow of death and my emergence into the light on the other side. This is my testament to the ability of humans to find their higher selves, even in times of terrible anguish. It is my life. I hope you'll find something in here that will help you in your own life—that you'll come to understand, as I have, that suffering ends when awakening begins.

CHAPTER 1

LETHAL
ICE CREAM

E ven now, more than forty years after the fact, I still have a hard time believing that my mother tried to murder my sisters and me. That event, obviously, changed my life forever. Initially, it put me on a downward path into the darkest place imaginable. Evil came into my world. Yes, I do believe evil exists, but it was only by passing through the darkness of evil that I was able to find the joy of being awakened in the light, and certainly, I also know love exists.

In April of 1973, I was a normal, eleven-year-old suburban kid. On the day it happened, even though it was the middle of spring, in Chicagoland it had only recently turned warm, and there were gray, slushy piles of snow on the roadsides. It was in the low fifties, and the dark sky promised rain.

The weather wasn't unusual for the Chicago area at that time of year, but this day was going to be special. At least that's what my mom said. We'd gotten up for school like on any other day, but much to my amazement, my mother had said we were going to see the Ice Capades at the old International Amphitheatre in Chicago.

Like any kid, I was over the moon with the thought that I didn't have to go to school. Even when we were sick, Mom insisted we go to school, so this was nothing short of amazing.

"Woo-hoo!" I shouted when she gave us the news. "No school today!"

"Really?" said my younger sister.

"You want to go see the show, don't you?" said Mom.

We all screamed with excitement and assured her that we did.

"I'm going to run out and get some gas so we don't have to stop on the way," said Mom. "Why don't you kids just relax and watch TV till I get back."

About an hour later, my mom pulled the car into the garage, and we heard the garage door close. I thought that was odd because we'd be leaving soon anyway. We lived in a split-level, and the garage was on the level above the family room.

We could hear her setting paper grocery bags on the counter, and then she came to the head of the stairs and called down to us. "Kids, you wait down there for a minute. I have a surprise for you."

I jumped up off the couch and headed for the stairs. "What is it?"

"Wait," she said. "I said you have to wait. If you come up too soon, you won't get the surprise. You hear?"

I went back to the couch, and my sisters and I giggled as we speculated about what the surprise could be.

"Okay, you three," Mom finally called down from the kitchen. "Today's going to be a special day. Who wants some ice cream before we leave?"

We were off the couch and up the stairs in a heartbeat. Mom had three bowls on the counter and was dishing up some ice cream. We squealed with excitement. But when I took a closer look at my bowl, I froze. It was covered with what looked like crushed up white candy.

"Wow!" I said. "What's this topping? One piece has an S on it."

Mom seemed disturbed somehow, and distant, but she continued to prepare the dishes of ice cream, so I thought little of it. Maybe she just had a lot on her mind. "The S means your special, and it's a special day today."

We all thanked her and went back downstairs to watched TV while we devoured the treat.

At first, my sisters didn't see any of the special bits in their bowls, but then they too found the pieces marked with an S.

A few minutes later, my mom came down the stairs with a blanket draped over her arm. In one hand she had a hammer, in the other a box of nails.

"What's that stuff for, Mom?" I asked.

She didn't respond. She just started nailing up the blanket across the entryway that lead into the family room. That shut out a lot of light, and the room immediately became stuffy. I thought I caught a faint whiff of car exhaust, but I didn't think anything of it.

"Mom why are you nailing up the blanket?"

She turned to me again. Her eyes were empty and almost lifeless. "It's a surprise for your daddy when he comes home from work."

I frowned. "What surprise?"

"Oh, you'll see."

I was bewildered at the time, but years later, when I looked back on the "surprise" she had in store for Dad, I realized the depth of her hatred for the man.

She went through the door from the family room to the garage, leaving the door open. I figured she must have left it open because we'd be leaving any moment. I hurried to finish my ice cream.

There was no sign of Mom for a while, and I started to wonder why we hadn't left yet. If we didn't hurry, we were going to be late for the start of the show. But now I was tired for no apparent reason.

Done with our ice cream, we just watched TV while we waited for Mom. My sisters lay on the floor with their pillows, and I stayed on the couch. I began to smell more exhaust fumes and thought I saw a faint bluish wisp drifting in from the garage. "I think the car is plenty warm now," I yelled toward the garage.

My mother didn't respond.

Now I began to feel more than tired. I was woozy, sleepy, and sick. The room was becoming foggy from the fumes billowing in from the garage, making it difficult for me to see the TV. My sisters seemed oblivious to the exhaust; they were sitting closer to the screen, but they did begin rubbing their sleepy eyes. The carbon monoxide burned my eyes, and I had to squint to get them into focus. I could taste the filthy exhaust as it coated the inside of my mouth and nose. My chest got tight, and I began to cough violently. I felt isolated—alone, and I wondered what was happening to me and hoping I wasn't going to have a full-blown asthma attack. I couldn't imagine why we were down here alone and why our mom wasn't here to help us.

On the floor, my sisters were gently rolling from side to side. They weren't saying anything, but each gave an occasional little whine or moan. Then they closed their eyes, and they seemed to be drifting in and out of sleep.

It was getting harder and harder for me to breathe, and I quickly realized an asthma attack was coming on. I didn't have my inhaler with me, but I didn't have the strength or alertness to get up and get it. Soon I was choking and coughing. I was gasping for air, but there was no clean air to be found.

Then a virgin thought entered my mind: This is what death feels like. I'm going to die. It wasn't some whimsical notion. I knew clearly that my time to die had arrived, and I surrendered to the fact.

Not only couldn't I breathe, I couldn't even manage to keep my eyes open. I was weak. My body was limp, and all I wanted to do was lie down and drift away. I felt like my whole body was wrapped in many heavy blankets, but through all those layers, I heard a voice. It shook the whole room, like rolling thunder. Not a pretend voice or some distant spirit voice. It was a real voice. I had no concept of such things at the time, but I know now that it was my higher self, speaking to me, guiding me. "Get up and go for the door. Go for the door!" The voice said. It was forceful but not angry or panicked. It was an encouraging voice, and I just did what it said. My response was automatic. I didn't think or question what I was being told. It was like the voice flipped a switch in me, and I just did as I was told, like a robot following a command.

The encouragement of the voice didn't end the lethargy, but it was enough to get me to my feet. I turned to the garage door and started to move. The door seemed to be a hundred yards away, but one step after another, I made my way toward it. I felt like I was wearing lead shoes and walking up a steep hill through chest-high water.

I tried to call out to my sisters, but all I could do was just breathe. Over and over, I gasped, trying to take in huge gulps of air, but the air in the room was dirty, and my efforts to breathe didn't seem to amount to much. When I reach out toward the door, my arms felt like concrete. I staggered and almost fell. But I managed to right myself. I knew that if I did go down, I might never get up again.

My legs trembled and my knees were about to buckle. My eyes burned, and I had to fight the urge to squeeze them shut against the pain. Now I was in a race with my own failing body. If I could get to the door before I collapsed, maybe I'd live through this.

And then it seemed like someone or something much greater and more powerful than me began controlling my limbs.

I could barely see the garage door through the fumes. I glanced back at my sisters, still motionless on the floor, their limbs in awkward positions. I wanted to go back, to try to rouse them, get them to come with me, but I knew I didn't have much strength—much life—left in me. If I didn't make it to the door, my sisters would surely be dead. I could easily have settled to the floor with them and closed my eyes. But I knew I never would have opened them again.

So I turned and faced the garage door again. I had to command my legs to take each step. But it felt like something other than my own mind and will was driving me. Whatever that great power was, without it, I wouldn't have continued.

That trip across the floor to the garage seemed to take an hour, but finally, I made it, still on my feet, still conscious, barely. But once inside the garage, I still had to climb four steps to get to the level the car was sitting on and then to the back door. The fumes in the garage were even thicker, a dark, dirty cloud. I could feel the oily exhaust on me like a heavy, filthy blanket. As I faced the steps, I grabbed hold of the wrought iron rail and steadied myself, but I realized to my horror that I didn't have the strength to climb the steps. My whole body was trembling. I would have burst into tears, but I didn't even have the strength to do that. I'd come all this way only to know that I could collapse here at the foot of the steps and die.

But something was pushing me, whether physically or just emotionally I can't say as I look back on that moment. With every tiny bit of strength that remained in my body, I lifted my left foot to the first step. I grabbed the railing with my left hand. Then I used my right hand to lift my right thigh, and I got my foot to the second step.

Now I was right next to the tailpipe of the car, the exhaust pouring onto me through the wrought iron railing like smoke from a raging fire.

I was choking and gagging. Two more steps to go. I slid my hand up the railing and pulled myself forward while lifting my leg to the third step. I stretched out with my arm, but the doorknob was out of my reach. Gasping for air and almost overcome by the toxic exhaust, I lifted my leg to the next step. Now I wrapped my fingers around the doorknob and used it to pull myself up.

My fingers, in fact my whole body was trembling as I reached for the latch and turned it. I pulled on the door, but that door always stuck. I had to pull with all my strength. For a moment I was afraid that if the door came open suddenly, I might fall backward down the steps I'd just climbed. I knew I couldn't make it up them a second time. But I had to get that door open. I felt like I was having a tug-of-war with the devil.

Finally, the door popped open. A wind gust of clean, fresh, cool air hit my face. I stood for a moment on the threshold between life and death, and then I staggered forward into the clean, crisp life.

But I realized the horror wasn't over. I was still dreadfully sick, and I needed someone to help me save my sisters. I tried to scream, but nothing came out. And it was the middle of a school day and work day. Even if I could find the strength and breath to scream, I knew no one was going to hear me, let alone help me. We had a six-foot privacy fence in our backyard. As far as the world was concerned, I was invisible. I wasn't going to make it. I was going to die, and my sisters were going to die if they weren't dead already.

Then I felt something from within me again. Some force, energy, or power—the same thing than had gotten me up off the couch and helped me all along the way. Even though I could barely hold myself up and was laboring for every breath, something told me to try one last time to call out for help. I steadied myself against the wall of the house and tried to fill my lungs with as much air as I could. I lifted my face to the sky and yelled, "Help!" It still wasn't loud enough to wake a sleeping baby, but it drained me. I was on the edge of blacking out.

At that moment, I felt something squeezing both my arms so hard they hurt. At first I thought it was just a side effect of the carbon monoxide poisoning. Then someone started shaking me so violently my knees buckled, and I knew I wasn't standing on my own.

Someone screamed, "Robert! Robert!"

I looked up at the person, but I was so disoriented that I couldn't make out the face or the voice. I finally managed to focus my eyes and was surprised to see that the person shaking me was my mother.

With the violent shaking and the screaming, my first thought was that she was angry that her plan had failed. I was terrified that she intended to finish me off.

But after she got over the fact that her plan had failed, she seemed to snap out of it. She sprang into action. She ran into the house, and I later learned that once inside she'd called my father at work and told him there'd been a terrible accident, that she'd forgotten to turn the car off after parking it, and the house was full of fumes. He told her to open all the windows, and he raced home. I don't remember his reaction when he reached the house, but I'm sure he was freaked out. He called his parents, and they came over. My sisters went to the hospital in an ambulance.

Today a mother who tried to murder her children would be put in jail, and the father would be a suspect as well. But this was the early '70s. There was no police response, no investigation, no charges filed. And there was no therapy for my sisters and me. Not for my dad either. People just weren't as aware back then. Society wasn't as aware.

CHAPTER **2**

REMAIN SILENT

There is a reason I am the way I am. My father never spoke of what my mother tried to do to my sisters and me. He was certainly deficient in communication skills and the ability to articulate his thoughts and feelings in a constructive, nurturing manner. Looking back, I can see that he was loving, albeit he didn't know how to express love. This, of course, was rooted in his own childhood. He was a lonely child, limited in his social skills, from a dysfunctional family. This resulted in low self-esteem and self-worth, which I inherited. I now understand that these problems can run for many generations if not recognized and addressed.

After the "event," my mom was hospitalized. I can only guess what kind of treatment she received back then. As for my dad, my sisters, and me, not only did we not receive any kind of counseling, we never even talked about it among ourselves. We swept it under the rug. I suppose we just hoped that with the passage of time, everything would be fine.

Though I never talked about it with anyone in the family, after I recovered from the effects of the carbon monoxide, a horrible emotional pain remained. But even greater than the pain was an extreme sense of betrayal that would grow inside of me like a cancer on my soul.

I became aware that my dad was not dealing with things very well one night at dinner a couple of weeks after the incident. My older sister was ragging on my younger sister about her schoolwork. "I can't believe how dumb you are," she said. "You just never pay attention. And do you even read the chapters you're supposed to?" Then she dipped her fingers in her glass and flicked water at my sister's face.

Dad suddenly just blew up. "Shut the hell up!" he yelled, and he slammed his fist down on the table, but he accidently hit the edge of his bowl of chili. Chili went flying everywhere, and that only enraged him more. He shot up from the table, knocking his chair over in the process. He grabbed his spoon off the table and flung it against the wall.

This was not unusual behavior for him. He was an angry, violent man. But it frightened and confused me. Why was he so angry? Did he love my sisters and me? Did he hate us as much as Mom seemed to?

It seemed like a year passed before my mom was discharged from the hospital, but it had only been a few months. I didn't know what to make of her presence in the house again, and I found myself walking on eggshells. I noticed everyone else was too. Was she stable? Was she going to snap again?

I didn't think about it at the time, but now I realize it was tough for her too—not knowing how her husband and children were going to welcome her back. But what reservations and fears we had about her we kept to ourselves, each of us living in a separate, private world of doubt. But we tried to go on like nothing happened.

I tried to make sense of the obvious fact that I had been the intended victim of a premeditated murder by my own mother. The best I could come up with was to tell myself it was some sort of a freak accident. Later I overheard my dad talking with his parents about the whole thing, and that ruined any lies I'd constructed, leaving only the cold reality I'd kept in the back of my mind all along.

That overheard conversation, and the new, angry behavior my father exhibited, just made everything worse. I felt worthless, unloved, a burden. Of course, I made myself feel that way by accepting his statements and his anger. That anger made me feel I was doing something wrong. In this environment, my thinking became corrupt. I created a pattern of negative thoughts that would haunt me the rest of my life.

CHAPTER 3

FAMILY
DYNAMICS

I can trace the problems in the family dynamic back to my parents' upbringings at least. Life in my immediate family was pretty wild. My parents argued and fought a lot. Maybe they weren't made for each other, but how could they possible have known.

Mom was raised on the South Side of Chicago, the second oldest of four kids. The other three were boys. She didn't get much education, but she was very creative. Her father died when she was eight. Her mother, a nurse, raised her and her brothers mostly on her own. She was sixteen when she got married and seventeen when she started having kids. She never had a chance to grow up.

My father was an only child and was not treated well by his parents. With their permission, he went into the US Marines early to get out of the house. And his childhood was definitely challenging. Still, he was a good guy.

When he wasn't drinking, it was easy to see he had a huge heart and a tremendous love for his children. And the man could build or make anything, from a room addition to a boat. He made a pontoon houseboat in 1966 when I was five. I remember watching him build it. When coming out of the cabin, there were only about twenty inches on each side—with no rails! It was very nerve-racking going out on the front deck while the boat was cruising down the river.

That boat was important to me, but there was another boat in my childhood that had even more special meaning.

My grandfather had a forty-five foot yacht, the largest one in the harbor, an awesome yacht, and I got to spend a lot of time on it. I would sit in the front and catch the breeze and the mist coming off the bow wake. Or I'd go up onto the sky deck and enjoy the sun and the 360 degree view.

The real excitement was on the weekends when the yacht club would have fish fries, and all the boats would tie up next to one another. People would go from boat to boat to get to the dock. It was one big party.

I loved cruising up and down the Illinois River. We'd beach the yacht at a spot called the sandpits so we could go swimming. We'd jump off the bow or the stern usually, but sometimes my grandfather let us jump off the sky deck. It was a fantastic time. I loved that yacht!

It was so calming and peaceful, a refuge from all the crazy stuff that went on in my childhood—the fighting between my parents, their anger toward me, what sometimes seemed to be their lack of love for me. On the yacht I quickly and easily forgot all my troubled family life. Thinking back now brings back memories of joy and serenity; those times really kept me together. A day on the yacht was like a shot in the arm of good times and happiness. It never lasted long enough though. I always longed to go back as soon as I could to get another fix. It was like a dream life, and it created a dream in me—that one day I would have a yacht of my own. I believed that having my own yacht would allow me to have all the peace and tranquility I needed. Somehow, having my own yacht would mean being truly happy, never having to worry about anything. Being on my granddad's yacht was a magic carpet ride. It was the closest thing I had to therapy, and it worked wonders while it lasted.

But when Granddad pulled into the dock after a day of peace, it was back to reality for me. When my dad drank, his anger would come to the fore. One day my sisters and I heard a commotion outside. I ran out the front door and saw Dad fighting with the neighbor, over what I don't know. They were wrestling on the bushes and punching each other. Dad ended up with a black and blue eye. I got scared. I didn't understand why he had to fight.

In the marriage itself, as the months turned to years, the relationship between my mother and father became more volatile, the yelling intensified, and there were even physical fights between the two of them. It made me timid, afraid of my parents and other adults.

I assumed I was the cause of some of these problems. It didn't seem people received counseling back then; you just dealt with problems the best you could and hoped things would turn out right. The majority of the time they didn't. I could count the times on one hand remembering being happy as a child.

My parents' relationship was troubled going back to long before I can remember. When I was a year old, my dad had kicked my mom out of the house because he thought she was having an affair. Dad swore to me he never touched my mom around the time my little sister would have been conceived. In fact, my little sister looks nothing like my older sister or me. Today, she insists that my father is not her father and that she knows who her real father is.

My parents separated again when I was five. That episode I do remember. My mom and my older sister and I moved to the apartment my mom's parents owned in a three flat on the South Side of Chicago.

The apartment in Chicago was always a little noisy because of the number of people in the house and the traffic outside. A separation like that is a shock to any child, and it certainly was to me, but there were things in my new life I enjoyed. I liked running up the stairs to the other apartments and playing outside. And there were a couple of kids I played with. But it was hard for me to make friends.

We lived with Grandma for about four months, and then my parents decided to get back together. As we packed up the car for the move back to our house, one of my few friends was hanging out with me. He was bummed out that I was moving. I was sad about it too. My friendships were few, and any refuge from my family life was a big deal for me. I wanted to continue to be his friend, but I wasn't sure how that would happen.

"Don't worry," I said. "We'll still be friends because you're nice to me. I'll let you buy me an ice cream cone." I don't know why I said that, exactly. It just seemed like it was appropriate to make a pact at that moment. But, actually, I never saw him again. It was just part of the chaos and instability of my life.

The day we moved to Rolling Meadows was unforgettable. I was running in and out of the house, carrying boxes in from the car, the smell of the cardboard and tape signaling the start of something new. At one point I set a box down on the living room floor and turned to run outside and get more. I put my hands out in front of me, like I was flying. Someone had just gone out and closed the glass storm door. My hands hit the glass, and it shattered, leaving my hands and fingers covered in blood. It was scary, for me and everybody else who saw it, but it wasn't as bad as it looked. With several Band-Aids, I was good as new. I was eager to begin this new chapter in my life, but maybe if I'd been older, I'd have understood the incident with the glass door as symbolic of the home life I'd have there. Really the same one I'd always had with my parents. It wasn't really a new beginning at all. It was the same old story.

In the winter of 1967, we were hit by one of the largest snowstorms in Chicago history. Nearly two feet of snow fell. Back then it always seemed to take a couple of days to dig out from a big storm before businesses, schools, and society would start functioning at a normal pace again. We were all stuck at home but doing what we could to deal with the effects of the storm. My dad was snow blowing the driveway near the garage, and I was his little helper, shoveling snow at the end of the driveway. The drifts were bigger than me. Each shovelful was heavy, and I was really struggling. I'd been at it for ten minutes or so when I lifted a huge shovelful and felt a sudden pain in my lower abdomen. I dropped my shovel, doubled over, and crumpled to the ground. As I lay on my side, I saw Dad coming toward me, leaping through the drifts like a deer. He scooped me up and carried me inside and called an ambulance. Somehow, that ambulance made it through all that snow and took me to the hospital. Mom rode with me.

The emergency room doctor told my mother I had a double hernia and needed surgery to repair it right away.

I was laying on an exam table surrounded by a curtain. Every time I moved, the clean, white paper on the table rustled. I was trying to stay as still as I could so I could hear what the adults were saying about me. The doctor and my mom were standing just outside the curtain. No matter how still I was, I still couldn't make out what was being said, but I could hear the doctor's cold, matter-of-fact tone. It was like he was talking about a wrecked car. Years later, my mom told me what he'd said. "Unfortunately, ma'am, due to your son's severe asthma, the situation is grave. He's not likely to make it through the surgery. If you want to do something, you might go ahead and pick out a coffin for your son. The odds are very slim he'll come through the surgery alive."

But I did make it. Somehow.

CHAPTER **4**

INNOCENT
FRIENDSHIP

In our new neighborhood, I still found it hard to make friends, but I had found one. My new friend, Tim, and I were exploring one day and wandered out of the neighborhood. We went into an apartment complex about eight blocks away from my house. I knew my parents wouldn't like that, but all I was doing was having fun. It wasn't like I was trying to get away with something. It was a totally innocent adventure. And it was a respite from my parents' behavior.

In this new and still-unexplored place, we met a very endearing and friendly lady. After we talked to her for a while, she invited us into her apartment to show us some interesting stuff she had. She was very kind. She showed us some drawings her husband had done of Peanuts characters. She fed us peanut butter and jelly sandwiches with milk. The sandwiches were stuffed with grape jelly, and I had to lick the edges of the sandwich to get some of it before it fell out. While we ate, she told us wonderful funny stories about her and her husband. We completely lost track of time, but finally we realized we'd been gone from our block most of the day. We thanked the lady for inviting us in and headed back home. On our way home, we talked about the lady, her funny stories, and the drawings she had. We were filled with the magic of the adventure we'd had.

I don't know what happened to Timmy when he got home, but when I walked into my house, my parents started yelling at me. The escape from their anger backfired on me.

"Where did you go?" said Mom. "Why did you just disappear like that? You should never go anywhere without telling us!"

"We did tell you," I said. "What did I do?"

Dad took his belt off and gave me a good whipping, the leather whistling through the air, making me cringe as I anticipated each lash. After that, he told me never to run off like that again, and he grounded me for four days.

My childhood asthma was debilitating, some months more than others. My playing outside and other activities had to be limited. One summer my asthma was so bad I could barely breathe outside. I was allergic to just about everything out there: grass, tress, mold, pollen, ragweed, etc. I spent a lot of time indoors in the air conditioning. Even then I had to get three allergy shots every week. But nothing could keep me indoors completely. With my inhaler by my side, I still rode my bike, swam, even played baseball and football. I was just a really adventurous kid. Throughout my childhood, I would go exploring in whatever neighborhood we lived in. And beyond. Once I rode my bike more than twenty-six miles round trip to visit a friend. My friends and I floated down the creek on rafts made out of Styrofoam. And we climb a lot of trees. Once we strung rope from one tree to another to make our version of a zip line. But that adventure didn't turn out so well. I fell ten feet onto my side and got the wind knocked out of me. I walked home, gasping for breath the whole way. My asthma wasn't going to stop me. When I got a little older, the condition of my lungs improved some, but still, it wasn't fun, and I found ways to be adventurous.

For a brief period when I was nine, Tim and I were infatuated with playing with matches. One day we were in the garage of my next door neighbor, Mrs. Geisler. Her lawnmower was in the back of the garage, alongside a gas can. Tim and I were lighting matches back there, not knowing about the deadly combination of gas and matches. Nothing happened at the time, but later that week, Mrs. Geisler was cleaning her garage and came across the matches. Timmy and I were constantly messing around her place, and she'd caught us sneaking into her garage before, so she knew it had to be us who'd left the matches there. So she went to see my mother.

When I got home, Mom told me Mrs. Geisler had come over.

"Really?" I said. "What did she want?"

"She wanted to give me these," she said. She held out a saucer full of burnt matches, and I immediately knew where they'd come from.

Then Mom took a new book of matches, peeled one off, and struck it. She grabbed my wrist, and stared at me for a moment. "You want to play with matches?" she said. "You want to play with matches?" She brought my hand closer and closer to the flame. She had a weird look in her eye. I was to see it again two years later on the day she tried to poison my sisters and me. A cold, vacant look.

"No! No!" I yelled. I could feel the heat of the flame as my hand got closer to it. "No!" I yelled one more time, convinced she intended to burn me.

She blew out the match. "Don't do that again. Now go to your room."

I ran to my room crying.

CHAPTER 5

BULLIES AND ANGELS

I n my environment, bullying happened all the time, and many times parents never even knew. You could be literally knocked unconscious by another kid, and still no one talked to their parents or teachers about it.

One day I was walking home from school, and I came across some kids playing by a bridge, throwing rocks in the creek. They started calling me names, and then they pushed me down the embankment of the bridge. I fell down by the creek and hit my head on a large rock and was knocked unconscious. I don't remember what happened after that, but I must have come to and walked home.

At home, my parents noticed right away something was wrong with me and took me to a doctor. He examined me and concluded that I had a concussion. He was amazed that I was able to make it home. "That boy is very fortunate to be okay," he told my parents. "Someone must have been watching out for him."

Of course, that's just something people say, but looking back, I really believe it. It's just one more example of a time when someone was looking out for me, taking care of me.

My life was plagued with accidents. Many of these should have killed me. They would have killed me if someone weren't making sure I didn't die.

In the summer of '72, we were on my dad's boat (not Granddad's unfortunately) on Fox Lake, in the Chain of Lakes, zipping across the water in our nineteen-foot runabout. It had a U-shaped bow, and my sisters and I would usually sit up there and enjoy the mist spraying on us to cool us down on those hot summer days. Dad would get the boat going so fast that we had to squint into the wind. I would usually wrap my arm around the railing so I could hang on when we went through the waves. My dad would drive around in circles, then cut the power. The bow would dip under the waves and swamp the front of the boat. My sisters and I would get drenched, and then we'd all yell, "Do it again!"

Boating and drinking seemed to go hand in hand in those days—on those lakes, at least. At some distance from us, my dad spotted a guy being very erratic—reckless, really—at the helm of his boat. Dad swore and turned us away from the other boat, but he still kept a sharp eye on it.

"Look at that crazy nut," he said. "He nearly ran into two other boats right there."

I turned so that I could keep an eye on it too. And then that boat turned right for us. The last thing I remember was being about twenty-five yards from it, and it was still headed right for us. My sisters and mom screamed, my dad swore, and then nothing. I was knocked unconscious for a short time. I don't remember the impact, but my arm was hit by the other boat when it crashed into us. Our boat's hull was torn open by the other guy's propeller. Everyone else was okay, but when I came to, I couldn't straighten my arm. I was afraid it was broken. An ambulance was called and I was taken to a doctor, again. The X-ray showed my arm was not broken, but the doctor wrapped it in an ACE bandage.

CHAPTER **6**

IMPACT OF
PARENTS' BEHAVIOR

I got in fights all the time as a kid. I guess I learned to fight from my parents. I couldn't get away from the incessant screaming and many times I went to sleep with a pillow over my head. When my dad would actually hit my mom, all I wanted to do was run away.

I didn't think it could get any worse between my parents, then my mom started working in a bar down the street. Dad really hated that. I think he was jealous of her being around any other men. So, yes, that did make things worse.

And things started to get worse in my behavior too. Although my mother did instill in me the belief that it was important to try to help other people, at a certain point that idea began to take a backseat to the more violent and negative behavior that started to manifest itself in me.

I became more rebellious and violent. I didn't even save it for school. I started getting in fights with the kids at the bus stop. There were two kids down the street that I had been friends with, but something happened, and we became bitter enemies. We used to make nasty comments to each another. We fought at the bus stop. This seemed to happen on a daily basis.

And it happened with other kids too. There were times when I knew I could hurt a kid really bad, but I chose not to do it. The fighting soon spread from the bus stop to school. I had been picked on in school, and originally I was egged on by the other kids to fight back. I wasn't very good at fighting at first, but when you get beat up enough times, you start to learn. It seemed like the other kids and I took our turns beating each other up.

One day at the bus stop, both of the brothers decided to jump me, so it was two against one. Although I was able to hold my own for a short time, they soon got the upper hand and were beating on me. On that day, my mom happened to be up early. After looking out the window, she came storming out of the house in her robe and slippers and threw one of the boys off me to break up the fight.

Later that week, the boys' parents came to our door to tell my parents they were going to sue us. They said my mom beat up their son. We ended up going to court a few months later. In his testimony, one of the boys said about my mom, "She sat on my back and beat me with her fist." Everybody in the courtroom started laughing. Everything about the case sounded so ludicrous that it was thrown out. The family moved out of the neighborhood shortly thereafter.

CHAPTER **7**

THE
DIVORCE

A couple of years after Mom came home from the hospital following her attempt to murder her children, she asked my dad for a divorce. To my surprise, my sisters wanted to live with Mom. I guessed it was just that most girls wanted to live with their mothers because they were girls, but I didn't really understand. I was now only thirteen, but I sure didn't want to live with my mom after she'd tried to kill me.

When my parents went to court for the custody hearing, my sisters didn't go, but I did. Maybe that was a mistake. The judge asked me where I wanted to live. I told him I wanted to live with my dad. I had thought I was pretty calm, but when I was confronted with actually having to express my choice, my calm was melted away by hot anger, and the anger didn't know where to go.

I turned to my mom and yelled at the top of my lungs, "You bitch!"

Then I jumped up and ran out of the courtroom, then the building, down the street, then into the next block. And I just kept running. I lost track of how long or far I ran, but at a certain point, I was just too exhausted to run anymore. I came to a staggering stop, bent over, and put my hands on my knees. Panting for air, I looked around to get my bearings. Then I realized I was in Chicago. I was on the west side of the city, but beyond that I really didn't know where I was, and I was a bit frightened. In addition to being physically exhausted, I was emotionally drained. I kept looking around, turning and turning to see if I could spot something I recognized. The noise of the traffic and people talking in loud conversation filled my head, and I felt nothing but confusion. I got to a pay phone and, by some small miracle, I was able to get connected to a phone in the courtroom and get somebody to put my dad on so I could speak to him. I read him a few businesses around me, and he told me to stay put and that he'd come pick me up.

After the divorce, Dad and I moved in with my grandfather, which was great. I loved hanging around my grandfather. When we were finally able to afford an apartment of our own, we found one in Granddad's building in the unit directly above his. We had no furniture and nothing in the fridge except my dad's six-pack of Budweiser. We slept on the floor for months.

My dad kept his love for me inside most of the time, but occasionally it surfaced. I think he was grateful I was sticking by his side.

I wasn't supervised much, so I was pretty much free to do what I wanted when my dad was at work. I met Larry, another kid in the same complex. One day when my dad was at work and Larry was over and we were in the bedroom, he looked in the closet and saw the BB gun my dad had used for target practice in our old yard when we lived in the suburbs. Larry picked up the gun, cocked it, and swung it around toward me. The gun went off, nailing me in the abdomen at close range. It hurt like hell and left a huge welt.

Larry looked at the gun, his eyes wide. Then he threw it on the bed. "I'm sorry," he said. "I didn't mean it. It just went off."

"It's okay," I said. "I think I'm okay, other than hurting like hell and having a divot the size of a pencil eraser in my abdomen."

What shocked me even worse was that Larry then picked up the gun, took careful aim at my chest, and pulled the trigger again.

A couple of months later, Larry and his family were kicked out of the building. The building management had good reason. Larry had started a fire in the storage lockers in the basement and tried to burn down the building.

CHAPTER **8**

LOSING MY INNOCENCE

I guess everybody assumes they have a normal childhood, but the truth is, we don't really have anything to compare to. Thinking back, I see that I had a lot of freedom for a kid my age. My dad was busy, or maybe he just didn't care. At our apartment complex, we had a clubhouse with a pool table. I used to spend hours down there every day after school. I was fourteen, and I became a very good pool player for my age. I could hold my own with anyone else in the building. I would usually play with Steve and Linda, a young couple who always seemed to be having relationship problems.

One day when Steve was out, Linda invited me up to their place. I sat in a ratty upholstered chair across from the couch. She got me a Coke and put on a Rolling Stones album. Occasionally she'd sing a line or two. When the song "Brown Sugar" came on, she looked at me and laughed, like the song was a big joke.

"You know what this song is about, right?" she said.

"I guess so."

She laughed again. "It's about a white guy going after a young black girl. Like he wants to do her."

I felt myself blush a little. I knew what the song was about, and it wasn't a big deal, but the way she talked about it and the look on her face made me uncomfortable.

"You know, you could sit over here next to me," she said, rubbing the couch cushion next to her.

I didn't know how to tell her I didn't want to do that, so I just chugged my Coke and sat there. I was starting to sweat.

"Do you want to come into the bedroom with me?" she said.

"I think I better go," I muttered, and I scurried out of the apartment.

My dad found another woman and in a few short months got remarried. I didn't really like that I had to take a backseat to her, and I decided to move back to my mom's. My dad was preoccupied with his new wife, and things around their place were hectic. At Mom's place things were calmer at least. That was mostly because she was waitressing and bartending to try and make ends meet and keep the house, so she was never home. She left around nine in the morning, and my sisters and I didn't see her until after eleven or so at night.

The cupboards and refrigerator were always empty. Mom would eat at the restaurant and rarely had food in the house or made any meals. There was usually a box or two of cereal in the house. We put powdered milk on it because we couldn't afford real milk. Occasionally we had hot dogs. Just hot dogs. No buns. No mustard. When my mom did bring any decent food home, it was from the restaurant. And most of that was stuff she dug out of the garbage cans or scraped off someone's plate.

I didn't like living this way, since I'd already been through sleeping on the floor and looking at the empty fridge in the early days at my dad's new place. Now that he was better off, I decided to go back and live with him again and his new wife, my stepmother. They rented a larger apartment in the same complex we'd been in. My grandfather had moved closer to Chicago, where he felt more in his element. That was where he'd grown up, and he always felt at home there. I remember him always in a faded shirt and polyester pants, constantly pushing his glasses up the bridge of his nose. He was a tough old Pole, who'd driven moonshine once or twice for Bugsy Siegel. He'd told me Bugsy was bad news—somebody you'd never want to mess with. So the streets of Chicago were just in Granddad's blood.

I started shooting pool again, but a lot of the faces in the clubhouse were new. There was a guy named Ben. He said he was a pilot and had his own plane. I thought that was really cool and never stopped to think it might be a lie. He said we should go for a ride sometime.

Sure. Why not? What could go wrong?

In those days, child molesters weren't on the internet. Now we can go online and see where sex offenders live. But when I was growing up, there could be a child molester right next door and no one would ever know. A lot of people didn't even talk about adults who molested children, but unfortunately, I became a target for child predators.

My friend Ben and I set a date and time to go up in his plane. That day, he knocked on my door, and I answered it. He was wearing dark glasses and a smile I could only describe as creepy. I suppose I sensed something wasn't quite right. But at that point in my life, I wasn't paying attention to my inner self. I didn't realize there was any wisdom in my soul or anything worth listening to in what my inner self had to say. I certainly didn't think I could rely on myself for guidance. I was always taught that help came from outside one's own soul. So whatever vibe I picked up on, I just shrugged it off as meaningless. And maybe my mom's attempt to kill my sisters and me made me numb to the intentions of others. It certainly devastated my sense of self-worth.

"Are you ready to go flying?" he said.

"Yes," I said.

My stepmother came up behind me and opened the door further and looked at Ben. "He's not going flying with you," she said. "Why were you taking a small boy flying with you when you didn't even ask his parents? What's wrong with you? This boy isn't going with you!"

She slammed the door. I couldn't believe she'd done that. She wasn't my mother. I wanted to go. Even though I was upset at my stepmother, she probably prevented me from being killed or at the very least sexually abused. I can't say for sure what his intentions were, but what kind of adult invites a young teen boy to go flying without asking the kid's parents? There was something definitely not right about Ben.

I decided to move back to my mom's again. I'm sure my stepmom really did want to bring me up in a good environment. She had raised two bright, well-educated, Christian daughters. She probably just assumed she could do the same for me. But I didn't realize she meant well. All I saw was someone trying to control me. I was uncontrollable, unruly, and had no respect for authority or any adults. I was still afraid of them, but I didn't really respect them.

Unfortunately, at Mom's I found that things were pretty much the same there as they'd been when I'd left the last time. When my mom was frustrated with me she would get the leather belt out and give me a few lashes. It would cause impressive welts of size and color on my arms and legs. It was painful, but in some sort of sick way my pain threshold went up, and it didn't seem as bad as it had in the past.

School was difficult for me, and it seemed too hard to keep my attention on learning. Reading and being able to comprehend what I read was challenging. I asked my sixth grade teacher, Mr. Null, what I could do to remember what I read. I told him I just couldn't comprehend what I was reading. He told me to pick out the words that jump out at me on the page and start from there. That really didn't seem to help me either.

High school was tremendously stressful. Not only was I having trouble academically, but I was still getting picked on constantly. But going into high school, I decided I was fed up with being bullied, so I began to fight back. When I was younger, the bullying and fighting had been different. That had all been between kids I knew and, in many cases, had actually been friends with at one time. We'd just gotten into calling each other names, and that had led to fights.

In high school, I didn't know most of the kids, and they were older. From the outset, I considered them serious threats. For the most part I only fought in self-defense. If other kids would start mouthing off or making fun of me, I'd stand my ground and talk back to them. Sometimes they'd come at me for that. And then I'd stand my ground and fight. But I always stopped short of inflicting a serious beating on anyone.

I started getting into more trouble as fighting became more prevalent in my life. My communication skills were extremely poor. I didn't want to open up to anyone or let them get close to me. I kept everyone at arm's length, sometimes by acting out in self-destructive ways that made just about everybody want to avoid me. I kept my thoughts and feelings to myself. I sort of had to, since I never had one good friend in high school. I didn't get close to anybody and didn't hang out with anyone I felt I could really trust.

Trusting and relying on others was something I avoided for a long time. Although I couldn't identify what was happening at the time, looking back it's pretty obvious. When the central figure in your life tries to kill you, then you trust no one. No one.

CHAPTER 9

RUNAWAY

There's a scene in the movie *Risky Business* in which Tom Cruise takes his dad's Porsche out for a drive while his parents are away. It was a bad move on his part, but at least he had a license. I did the same thing with no license and no idea how to drive. And in my case, it wasn't a Porsche, it was a '73 Plymouth Valiant. It was March 1976. I had a friend in Schaumburg named Dave. He and I used to shoot pool and hang out when I lived with my dad. He came over to my mom's in Palatine one weekend to spend the night. By this time, my mother wasn't home very often, but even when she was home, I wasn't listening to her much. I just did whatever I wanted. Dave and I were only fifteen, but we decided to take my mom's car out for a spin that night.

I thought we could take it for a quick drive and bring it back and she would never know. So we waited for her to go to sleep. Once we were sure she was asleep, we crept into the garage. Since it was directly under her bedroom, we opened the garage door as quietly as possible, cringing and stopping at every creak. Then we eased open driver side door, and I reached in, put the key in the ignition, and turned it just enough to unlock the steering wheel and the gear shift lever. There was no way I could have started the car in the garage without waking her. We put the car in neutral, left the lights off, and rolled it down the thirty-foot driveway and into the street. Even the sound of road grit under the tires made me look over my shoulder to check my mom's window for a light. Finally we got in, and I fired it up.

We drove around the neighborhood laughing and spinning through the dial on the radio, picking up music by Bad Company, The Eagles, and Marshall Tucker. When Bachman Turner Overdrive's "You Ain't Seen Nothin' Yet" came on, I couldn't help but step on the gas a little harder. I was having a blast, but I had no idea what I was doing, and it was a bit unnerving trying to aim the car down the middle of the road. We ventured out a little farther and farther from my home, eventually taking the car out onto some main roads. We ended up about seven miles from the house on Cuba Road, a road made notorious by a number of haunting stories local kids always told about it. It was a cool place to drive during the day because it had very steep hills. It was like riding on a roller coaster. Some of the drops were so steep they would throw your stomach into your throat.

At night it was spooky, not very well lit, and sparsely populated. The homes sat far back from the narrow road. Some of the tall, old oak trees had branches that hung over the road. I decided it would be really cool to get airborne going over these hills. The first time I tried it, we didn't get airborne, but we could feel the car's suspension clanking as the car was lifted as far as possible while the wheels were still on the ground. As soon as we left the crest of the hill on the down slope, the car was slapped back down onto the frame, and we bounced up and down in our seats, nearly hitting the ceiling.

The next time, I went a little faster, and this time we did get airborne. And came down harder. The next hill was the big one. I got it up to almost fifty miles an hour in a twenty-five mile an hour zone. We hit the top of the hill and went flying. We came down hard on the two right wheels and went into a barrel roll. The sound the car made was something I'd never heard before. It was a horrendously crunching, screeching, rumbling sound. I thought the car would be ripped apart before it came to a stop. Neither of us had our seat belts on.

When we finally did come to rest, I said to Dave, "Are you okay?"

"Yeah," he said. "How about you?"

"Other than my leg being caught in the steering wheel, I think I'm okay. Let's get out of here!"

We didn't wait for the police, and I don't even recall looking at the condition of the car. It was too dark to see much anyway. (We heard later that a man out walking his dog that night told the police we'd rolled about a hundred and fifty feet—half the length of a football field.)

We walked aimlessly for a while, a bit dazed and sore from the accident.

"What are we going to do now?" said Dave.

Instantly I knew I couldn't go home, nor did I want to. "I don't know about you, man, but I'm taking off."

"What do you mean, taking off?"

"I'm splitting town. I don't know how my mom's going to react to this, and I'm not going to stick around to find out. She'd probably kill me if I went home, and I'm not kidding. I'm going to Florida."

We parted then, and that's the last time I saw Dave. I got back out to a main road and started hitching to Florida. I had twenty bucks in my pocket. It was the only place I could think to go that was far enough away from my mother. I didn't really know the place, but my dad and I had been there before, and I still remembered a little about it, and I had fond memories of our time there.

CHAPTER **10**

SLIDE TO HELL

Sometimes when you're a kid you do things that put you in real danger, but you don't even know how dangerous they were until much later. I think back on the things I did and the people I lived with, and I wonder how I could have been so naïve. But I think I wanted to see the best in people.

The innocence and naïveté that I carried with me would disappear like smoke from a used match. It would be replaced with street smarts. But this came at a cost I hadn't really wanted to pay. Nobody would. I didn't even think about how I was going to support myself, what I was going to do to eat, where I was going to sleep. I'd left Illinois with nothing more than the clothes on my back and twenty dollars in my pocket.

On the trip down to Florida, I lost track of time. The road and the hitchhiking seemed endless. I'd walk for a while with my thumb out, then somebody would pull over for me. I don't recall sleeping the whole trip down. I met, let's just say, some very interesting people.

One trucker said he had to eat, so we stopped at a little diner right off the interstate and sat at a speckled Formica table. I ordered the cheapest hamburger they had, not knowing how long I'd have to make my money last. We sat at a table against the window, and between huge bites of his large bacon cheeseburger, he started asking me questions.

"Where are you going?"

"Florida."

"How much money do you have?"

I smirked. "I *did* have twenty bucks before I got this," I said holding up my little burger, now half eaten.

I wasn't sure why he was asking me. I thought maybe he was going to rob me. Instead, when it came time to pay the check, he said, "I'll take care of it. You're going to need your money."

He seemed to want to help me—for the time he was with me. But a few hours later, when it came time for him to turn off the interstate for his destination, he let me out of his eighteen-wheeler with a simple goodbye, and then I was on my own again.

Somehow in about twenty-four hours I had hitchhiked all the way down to my destination, Daytona Beach, Florida. Now what?

I remember walking by the airport that my dad and I landed at, not too far from the big fronton—the place where they play jai alai.

Eventually I made my way down to the beach were my dad and I spent a lot of our time when we were there. It had miles and miles of beautiful white sand. One of the greatest things about that beach was that they let people drive on it. The place was bustling with activity. Besides all the people laying out in the sun, splashing in the surf, and walking on the hard, wet part of the sand, there were people lazily drifting up and down the beach on motorcycles and in cars.

I hung out and people watched for an hour or so, and then I realized how hungry I was. I walked up off the beach to a McDonalds. Outside there were a lot of people hanging around who were not very well groomed. They were actually kind of a troubling crowd.

One guy was sitting on a bench holding a Doberman pinscher. He caught my eye and lifted his chin to me. "Where you from, kid?"

"Chicago."

"I'm Russell," he said. "What's your name?"

"Rob."

"So, Rob, where are your parents?"

I shrugged. "Chicago."

"You just up and left, huh?"

"Yeah?"

He shook his head and petted the dog. "Kid, you don't want to be down here. This is not a place for a kid. You're going to age too quickly."

Age too quickly? What was this guy talking about? I didn't give the advice any weight because I just plain didn't understand it.

We talked for a while and then he introduced me to the Dobi, Max. I petted the dog as it panted in the Florida sun. Russell just watched me for a minute, and then he sighed. "Rob, go home. I'll buy you a ticket on the next bus to Chicago."

I thought, Wow he doesn't even know me and he would do that? But *naïve* as I was, I told him no thanks. "I just got down here. I'm not going back home."

He didn't say anything. He just shook his head and gave Max a few pats on the ribs.

That night I slept on the beach right below the boardwalk. The next day I walked along the beach and checked out some of the area attractions. The town had a lot of action. There always seemed to be something to do. The only problem was that I only had a few bucks left in my pocket, and I was hungry. I spent the rest of my money on a bag of chips and pop. I didn't care much about nutrition back then. Even back home I usually only ate once a day, and it was only usually a bag of chips or a hot dog. Since I wasn't used to eating a lot, my current diet wasn't that much of a transition. I did what I could to get money, even if it was panhandling. One of the arcades on the boardwalk had a pool table. Even though I had no money to cover a bet, several times I played for money to buy food. First, I watched who was playing and made certain I could beat them. Then I would ask them to play. Usually, it was an unsuspecting tourist.

A couple days later, I came across the Russell on the boardwalk. He had Max with him. "How ya doing, kid?" he said.

"I'm okay."

"Did you have something to eat today?"

I shook my head. "No, not yet."

"You hungry?"

I told him I was, and he offered to buy me lunch. "I want to talk to you anyway."

If all I had to do to get something to eat was talk, I was all for it. We ended up at some off-brand sandwich place with tables outside under umbrellas. I ordered an Italian sandwich. When we sat at the table, I asked if I could give some salami to Max, and Russell nodded and smiled.

"If you want food and a place to sleep, I can help you out with that," said Russell.

"How?"

"It's no problem," he said. "Just come on over to my place."

I'd only been on the street a short time, but I was beat, so I said okay.

He lived in a town called Holly Hill, just north of Daytona Beach, and really, the south end of Holly Hill was right across from the Daytona Beach Boardwalk. His place itself was only about ten minutes from the beach.

When we got there, the house was full of people of all different kinds. There were several runaways and other guys who lived there. Some of them looked like typical stoners, druggies, and hippies. They were like something straight out of a movie from that time—the '70s. They all had long, stringy hair and were scrawny and badly put together. Some guys were shirtless. Some wore board shorts. Others were in faded and frayed jeans. Though a lot of people wore jeans like that at the time, on these guys it didn't seem like a fashion statement. I got the impression they were dressing as well as they could.

Russell and Mickey, another guy who lived there, trained Dobermans as guard dogs, so there were a few other Dobis around. Mickey was from Canada and was in his late thirties or early forties. He seemed out of place there. He was more straight-laced and clean-cut than everybody else. He slept in the garage. Inside the house, all the rooms were being shared except for Russell's room. It was his place, so he had his own room. I slept in the living room on the foldout sofa because all the other rooms were taken.

I hung out there for a couple of days doing more or less nothing. And then Russell sat me down and talked to me. "You have to start earning your keep, kid. I'm going to tell you how you can do it. All I want you to do is deliver this stuff for me."

I had no idea what he was talking about. "What stuff?"

"This grass I have. You take it to the people I say, and I'll let you sleep at my place and feed you."

That seemed okay to me. It wasn't like I was dealing drugs or anything, just dropping it off.

Then a few days later, Russell wanted to have another talk with me. "You know, when you're out, like on the boardwalk or wherever, you can just start asking people if they want to buy this grass. If they look like they might smoke, just walk up to them and ask them if they want to buy some weed."

If I wanted a place to sleep and food to eat, this was what I needed to do. So I did. The concept of morality didn't mean anything to me back then.

There was also a guy named Lenny in the house. A lot of guys went into the bedroom with Lenny when they came over. Lenny was probably in his thirties. He always had his door closed, and occasionally I would see boys I knew from the beach going in there. I always wondered what was going on in there and why he brought these other young boys around. It really was a weird scene.

On the beach one day, I came across three guys in a dark green '68 Galaxy 500. They said they wanted to check out what kind of weed I had, and they told me to jump in the car with them. We drove down Daytona

Beach for a while. They didn't say much. The driver reminded me of Charles Manson. He had an ungroomed beard and scraggly, greasy black hair that came down past his shoulders. The other two were grungy blonds. They all looked like acid freaks to me.

After being in the car for a few minutes, I noticed a terrible odor that started making me dizzy. I was feeling a headache coming on. These guys had their hands up to their face, and they were sniffing loudly. I recognized the scent of model car glue. They were all stoned, their eyes glazed over. I was getting a little nervous. I asked them if they wanted to buy any weed, and they said no.

I just wanted to get out of the car and away from that strong odor. After what seemed like half an hour, they finally stopped. One of the guys said, "Let him out."

I climbed out of the car practically gasping for the fresh, salt-scented air coming up off the ocean. The whole episode reminded me of the fumes that had almost killed me on that hellish day in my basement when I was eleven.

I told Russ, the guy who owned or rented the house, the story about the glue sniffers. He got it into his head that I needed some protection. There was another guy crashing at the house who seemed tough, so Russ put the two of us together and told the guy to watch my back.

I said to Russ, "I don't need this guy to protect me. I can take care of myself." I wasn't being entirely realistic. I felt like a big guy, but I was really only five-foot eight and about 125 pounds.

My would-be bodyguard was about my age, but he was six five. Russ thought the guy's size alone would make someone think twice about messing with me. I argued with Russ and wanted to kick this guy's ass. Despite my rant, the next day this goon and I started hanging out together.

We talked to some guy on the boardwalk, and he said he wanted to take us to meet his friend who was working at a restaurant about a mile away. So we all got in the guy's car and headed down the street. The goon sat in the front seat, and I sat in back.

The guy driving pulled into the parking lot of an Italian restaurant, but I thought it was odd to be meeting someone working there, because the place was closed. I figured maybe the friend was cleaning up after the shift or something. The driver pulled around the back. He brought the car to a stop in the middle of the blacktop, not in any kind of parking space. Then he pulled out a revolver and pointed it at the goon.

He looked at me, then the goon, then back at me again. "Okay, boys, hand it over," he said.

I scoffed. "We don't have anything."

The goon looked scared, but I was eager for him to grab the gun so we could jump on this guy and knock some sense into him. The goon handed over his bag of weed without even batting an eyelash. This was the guy who was supposed to protect me. Great!

For a moment, I thought about reaching over the seat and grabbing the gun. I was pretty sure I could do it. But I wasn't absolutely sure I could get control of the gun before the goon got shot. So as slowly as I could, I handed over my bag too.

"Get the hell out of my car!" the guy yelled.

We got out of the car and stood on the blacktop in the dark behind the restaurant and listened to the guy peel out of there. When he was gone, I turned to the goon. "What the hell were you doing? Why didn't you jump on that jerk? You had the perfect angle. You could have gotten the gun easy. And we could have taken him. What were you thinking?"

"I got scared," he said.

"Scared?" I shouted. "Scared? You're supposed to be protecting me. What a joke!"

After that, Russell decided to leave me on my own, and he assigned the goon to some other runaway who was crashing at the house.

CHAPTER **11**

DISCONNECTION
AND CONSEQUENCES

After I had my weed ripped off by a guy with a gun, I realized I was in an environment where anything could happen. It was a dramatic moment, but seemed like just one notch up from other stuff that had been happening in my life. I decided I didn't want to take any shit off anybody anymore. I was tired of it. The night after I got ripped off, I was hanging out downtown near the bars with about a half dozen guys from the house, including Indian. I called him that because he reminded me of Chief Bromden from *One Flew over the Cuckoo's Nest*. He was big and strong and didn't speak very much, just like the guy in the movie. We heard on the street that a girl who was part of a loose confederation of runaways, street kids, and misfits had been sexually assaulted earlier that day by some guy. People were talking about it, and we got a description of the guy and his car. We knew him. He was a local and a real scumbag. He was a scrawny, dirty guy who was always messing with people, always trying to put one over on somebody. He had a real reputation as a guy not to trust for anything. So we started looking for him. As we were walking by a bar, a guy came out the door and nearly bumped right into me. He looked like the guy we were looking for. I turned around and said, "Hey, you!"

He recognized me and knew I was a friend of the girl, and he took off running. I took off after him, but he darted around a corner, and I lost sight of him immediately. I yelled out to a few of the buddies, and we all charged after him. But before we even reached the corner of the building, a beat-up '69 Impala came screeching around the corner from the other side of the building. I turned and looked at the car and yelled, "It's him!"

There was this old fence pole that had once held up part of a fence in this parking lot. The fence was long gone, but the post remained, loose but still encased in a shell of concrete in the cracked asphalt. Indian grabbed the post and started working it back and forth until it broke free. He picked it up like a spear with a big hunk of concrete on one end. As the car approached, he chucked this pole from the sidewalk at the passing car. It just missed the car, soaring in front of the windshield and landing on the sidewalk across the street. I was amazed that he not only got it out of the ground but threw it like he did.

"Man," I said. "You almost had him. How did you throw that thing?" It must have weighed thirty pounds.

We heard the guy was eventually caught that night by the cops. He was lucky they got to him before we did.

It had only been about four weeks since I'd left home. I didn't realize it, but things were starting to take a toll on me. I had a friend back in Palatine named Cory. Surprisingly, he and his girlfriend came down to try and get me to come back home. I guess you never know how people really feel about you until something happens. As I said, I didn't really get close to anybody in high school, and I sure didn't know there was anybody I hung out with who cared enough about me to spend all their time and money to come down to see me. Cory and I knew each other through my older sister, and I guess something about knowing her first and then meeting me meant something to him. Anyway, somehow we were closer than I'd thought. Maybe they were just coming to Florida for their own reasons and decided to stop by. Cory's girlfriend, Jenny, was somebody we'd both had the hots for, but he had a car. I didn't.

They came to the house I was staying at. It wasn't hard to find. They just asked some street kid on the boardwalk and he told them exactly where it was. That night, they decided to stay with me. They were freaked out by the place and felt uncomfortable. They'd never been anywhere quite like it. There were drugs all over the place, people coming in and out, and guys coming out of the shower naked. It was a very casual, crazy place. For whatever reason, that night Jenny crawled in bed with me. I was a little confused by this, since I thought she was going out with Cory. I couldn't imagine she wanted to make love, because Cory was right next to us sleeping on the floor. Maybe she didn't really want to have sex. Maybe she just wanted to let me know I was loved—that there was somebody who would be there for me.

The next day they pleaded with me to come home with them.

I said, "I can't go back home. My mom will kill me." Even though that might have been true, there was a part of me that wanted to go home. In the end, I couldn't face my mother or think of what would happen if I did go back. I walked them to their car and thanked them again for coming down. They asked one last time before they drove off if I'd come back with them. They swore everything would be okay.

"I can't do it," I said.

This was a case of me not being able to hear what I was being told by my higher self. These were two people who really cared about me. I didn't get that because I couldn't fathom that such people existed in my life. I shut off my ability to perceive that.

I should have gone, or followed after them, before things turned worse. I was very confused; even though I hung out with these two I didn't think we were that close for them to care about me enough to drive down to Florida to try to get me to come back. At the time, on a scale of one to a hundred, sadly I thought I was pretty much a zero in the eyes of anybody I'd hung out with. I thought their coming down for me was just a prank.

I was so out there and disconnected, not only from my friends and literal reality, but from my true self. I couldn't understand why someone would want to love me or care for me. It's not that I couldn't understand—it's like the thought of someone loving me didn't exist. It wasn't possible.

CHAPTER **12**

LEAVING
HELL

Sometimes it happens that you think you're at your lowest point, and then you go a little further down. In Florida, I went about as far down as any person can go. It began when I came out after taking a shower and discovered the ragged clothes I'd been wearing were gone. Someone had stolen all of my clothes—even my underwear! I couldn't believe this, and no one admitted that they took them or even that they saw who did. I didn't think it was a prank. I just thought they were too stoned to remember. I had to borrow a pair of jeans and a T-shirt from someone else, but they didn't fit.

Having no money and barely eating was wearing on me. And with no clothes on top of everything else, what was I going to do now? The guy I borrowed the clothes from said he wanted them back soon.

There was that mysterious room in the house where the door was always closed, and the other boys I knew from the McDonalds where a bunch of us hung out were occasionally there. They never told me what was going on in that room. They only said that if I ever needed help, Lenny would take care of me. Lenny had an expensive convertible, and he was always driving around with boys my age. Some were locals, some runaways. I wasn't sure if he lived there or just came and visited. I'd never seen him coming or going. The young boys he was with always seemed well fed and well dressed. When we were at the hangout, some of these same boys said they didn't like Lenny.

I hadn't been eating. I didn't have money for food because I was tired of selling weed. So I thought I'd knock on the door of that mysterious room, and maybe Lenny would loan me some money so I could get some clothes and eat. I listened at the door for a moment, and when I didn't hear anything, I knocked. It took a minute, but Lenny opened the door in his shorts.

I asked if I could talk to him for a minute, and he said sure. I told him Marty had said I should come see him if I ever needed help. I explained to him that someone had stolen all my clothes. Since no one else would help me, I had nowhere to go.

He said, "Sure, I'll help you. Meet me outside by my car in an hour."

I was relieved, and an hour later, I stood out by the car and waited.

A few minutes later, he came out. He told me to hop in and he'd take me to get a pair of Levi's. He drove me to the mall with the stereo blasting. When Grand Funk's "American Band" came on, he started singing along.

As he parked he said, "When we go inside don't walk by me."

I looked at him, puzzled.

He read my thoughts. "People know me. Just walk ahead of me. Go find a pair of pants, put them on the counter, and then I'll go in the store to pay for them."

I thought that was odd, but it was obvious he had a plan, a system. I realized he must have done this many times before. I did as he instructed, and after I'd gotten my new clothes, we got back in the car and he started to drive. He drove for more than an hour and ended up at a house out in the middle of nowhere. He put the car in park, then turned to me and said, "You wanted me to help you, didn't you?"

"Yes."

"Now you're going to have to do something for me too."

"Like what?" I said.

"Let's go inside."

I followed him into the house, down a hall, and into a bedroom. He told me to sit on the bed.

"What?"

"Sit on the bed. You and I are the only ones here, and no one else is going to hear you. You needed new pants, right? You have no money, no food. I helped you, right? I didn't hurt you, but now it's time for you to do something for me. You trust me, don't you? I'm not going to hurt you." Then he unbuttoned my pants.

"Lay back on the bed," he said.

When I hesitated, he pushed me, and I fell back onto the bed.

"I'm not going to hurt you. You're going to like it."

Then the unthinkable happened to me. I'd heard about children and teenagers being molested, but to find that it was happening to me was surreal. The fact a man would do this to me made no sense. After this incident, I was very confused about what had just happened. I had just became another victim of what I later realized was a notorious pedophile. I found myself riding in his car like the other boys before me had done. I realized they must have all have been molested by this man too.

Abuse is a commodity. Lenny wasn't above selling me to someone else, and years later I would come to understand what a deprived person he was. Very early the next morning, Lenny said he wanted to take me somewhere and meet someone. I was shaken by the events of the previous day, but I said okay.

We drove south out of town and along the ocean for a good part of the morning. We came an area of what looked like million-dollar beach homes. We pulled into the driveway of one of the largest ones and went inside.

"I'll be back in a minute," Lenny said, and he left me in the front part of the house.

The place had a loft and was wide open. I could see all the way to the back of the house. I waited by the front door and saw him talking to a man. The guy looked like he was in his fifties with salt and pepper hair. He was about five nine and 170 pounds. He was in a white bathrobe and had a drink in his hand. The man looked very familiar, like some celebrity I had seen on TV. It just might have been a coincidence, but I could have sworn I'd seen him on TV.

After they'd talked for a few minutes, they both came up to the front of the house. The man walked right in front of me, and before I could even say hello, he slapped me right across my face. "You shit," he said.

I had no idea what I'd done to piss him off or what had just happened. I turned to Lenny, confused.

"Don't worry about it," he said. "It's time to go."

My best guess was that Lenny had told the guy that I wasn't a virgin, and that had angered him. He wanted a virgin. I came to realize that a lot of pedophiles do. It might very well be that Lenny's sexual abuse of me saved me from something more terrible.

Later that week I was hanging around near the house and saw a police car pull up outside it. I hid behind the neighbor's house first, then I ran behind a few houses, wanting to look to see if it was a bust but not wanting to get caught. A cop got out of the car. Then a lady got out.

I couldn't believe my eyes. I had to look closer. It was my mother! As soon as I saw her, I ran and hid behind another house where I could get a better view. The officer and my mom went inside the house. I watched for about ten minutes, and then my mom and the cop came out, got back into the police car, and drove away.

After that, I decided to stay away from the house for a few days. I didn't really want to stay at that house anyway, because of Lenny, but he actually wasn't spending much time there.

It had been nearly three months since I'd left home. Since I decided to leave the house, I went to stay with a guy I'd met at the boardwalk, and we hit it off pretty good. We met a couple of girls and tried to hook up with them. They said to come and look them up when we were in Palm Coast. We hitched up there and looked all day, knocking on doors on the street where we thought they lived. We never did find them. As the sun was going down, we started heading back.

It was almost June. Before I ran away, one of the last conversations I had was with my older sister. I didn't see her very much, but she said, "Wherever you are when I finish high school, you better be at my graduation." It was just about time for that. So I told my friend I was taking off.

"Where are you going?"

"I'm going back home. I've had enough."

I left Florida the same way I left Illinois—hitchhiking. I'd had enough of this lifestyle. I didn't like what I had become. I despised myself even more than ever before. Nobody wanted to pick me up. Russ had been right. I'd had no idea what he meant when he said the place would age me. Now I understood. When I considered my relatively short time in Florida, it felt like I was looking back over a lifetime. The night I crashed my mom's car and decided to take off, I was filled with a sense of adventure. Now I felt empty.

It seemed like I walked almost all the way to Chicago. I made it up as far as northern Florida, near Jacksonville. It was late at night. I was tired, hungry, and I had not been successful in getting a ride for some time. Somehow I ended up on a bridge. It seemed like I was walking on it forever. I didn't know there were bridges this long. There were not many cars out that night. The ones that were out just passed me by, one after the other. I was just hoping no one would hit me, since there was not much room to walk on the bridge.

Finally a car stopped about fifty yards in front of me. I started running toward the car, but then I slowed down as I began to make it out in the dark. Then roof lights came on and lit up the night in blue and red. I stopped in my tracks as a cop got out of his car and started walking toward me. I looked behind me, then in front, then behind me again; if I ran he would surely catch me. Then I looked down, it looked like it was only about thirty to forty feet straight down to the dark water.

I looked down again, contemplating making the jump. I grabbed on to a steel pole and was going to pull myself up onto the guard rail. Then I glanced up at the cop walking toward me. Then, down again. I couldn't even see clearly all the way down, and I didn't have a clue how deep the water was or how long the fall was. I figured I'd been running long enough. I was tired, and I was tired of running.

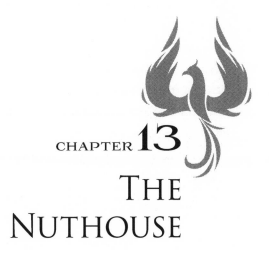

CHAPTER 13

THE
NUTHOUSE

The cop was really big and had me turn around. The blue and red lights from his squad car strobed off the bridge and the railing as I faced the darkness. "Where you headed?" he said.

"Home."

"I can take you home," he said. "Where do you live?"

"Chicago."

He chuckled. "Well, I can't take you that far." He searched me. Then he put the cuffs on me and asked me politely to get in his squad car. He took me to the juvenile correction center in Jacksonville.

There, he locked me in a cell, gave me a meal, and told me he was going to call my mother and make arrangements for me to get back home. He put me on a plane home the next day. My three-month escapade was finally over.

My mom picked me up at the airport in an old beater of car. Much to my surprise, she was glad to see me.

"What do you want do first when we get back home?" she said.

"I want to get back to school. Let's go to the high school." I was a sophomore.

"School?" she said.

"Yes, I want to go now."

So right from the airport, we went to Fremd High School. There were only a few weeks left of school, but I wanted to go back for some reason. I wanted to get some sort of normalcy back in my life as soon as possible.

When we got there, being around all those kids made me feel strange. I felt like everyone was looking at me. I was sure the news spread throughout the school that I had split. I wanted to fit in, but I didn't feel like I belonged there any longer. At school, all the frivolous crap, drama, and gossip people were involved in was so insignificant compared to what I'd been through. Regardless, I went back to school, but it wasn't easy. It was even more difficult than before.

One night I was hanging out with a guy I knew from the neighborhood. We weren't really friends exactly. Certainly not close friends. But he had just become a guy I hung out with. He was a trouble maker. I guess that's why we hung out. By that time, that was who I was too. We were just downstairs lifting weights, listening to music.

When she got home from work, Mom came downstairs and asked my friend to move his car so she could pull in the garage.

"When we're done," I said. "Then he'll move it." And I just went on with my set.

I remembered all of her behavior—beating me with a belt, yelling at me. But I was no longer afraid of her. A couple of days later, she brought up the subject of me mouthing off to her in front of my friend. She decided I need a beating with the belt. I didn't run. I just stood there and took it. I felt the intense pain on my arms and back, but I just watched her get enraged. She swung the belt and swore at me until she was exhausted and couldn't do it anymore. That was the last time I recall my mother whipping me with the leather.

I wasn't sure my dad was aware I'd run away from home until he mentioned it one day out of the blue. He didn't seem to be too concerned about it. His lack of ability to express compassion for me was disturbing.

I was sixteen now, and my mom had no idea how to handle me any longer. One night she told me to come downstairs. She wanted to talk to me. I never talked to my mother, and she almost never wanted to talk to me. Why would I want to talk to her or anyone about any problems I had. I didn't really think I had too many problems. I thought everyone else did. I could take care of myself and didn't need anyone to help me anymore. I went down to talk to her and saw that my uncle Gary was downstairs too. Gary was my mom's youngest brother. He was not tall but stocky—maybe five eight and 265. He was a clean-cut navy guy with a great sense of humor, and he could be loud sometimes.

My mom said, "I'm glad you came down. I decided we're going to admit you to a psychiatric hospital to get you some help."

I stared at her. "There is no way I'm going into a hospital! I don't need any help from anyone. I'm not crazy!"

"I thought you would feel that way," she said. "That's why your uncle's here. You're going."

Uncle Gary was a good guy, and we got along just fine. But he was there to do his sister a favor, and he was going to do it. He wasn't disrespectful of me. He was just businesslike.

I started to think about how I was going to get out of there, and I started to move around. But Gary followed me everywhere in the house. When I went into the bathroom, he made me leave the door open and waited at the door. He had his hand on the door jamb while I was in there taking a leak. I thought I could turn around and slam the door, push him aside, then bolt down the stairs and take off running, but that didn't happen.

He put me in his car and tied my hands together so I couldn't open the door and jump out. When we were getting off the ramp from the expressway close to the hospital, I thought I could jump out of the car even with my hands tied. It would have been hard because I wouldn't be able to protect myself, but I was thinking about it. Uncle Gary must have seen the gears turning in my head. He grabbed my left upper arm and held me for the rest of the drive.

The hospital was located in one of roughest neighborhoods in Chicago. I'm sure they did that for good reason—so no one would want to escape from there.

It wasn't like *One Flew over the Cuckoo's Nest*. Not that crazy. There were girls, boys, and young kids all in the same unit. They all seemed "relatively normal." Everything was locked down like a prison. The doors were locked, and security guards were stationed at the entrances and exits, and everyone had to have identification when they were coming and going. They told us when to sleep, they told us when to wake up, they told us when to eat, they told us when we could go outside. And I told them to fuck off and leave me alone. I was spending time in solitary confinement, which was an empty room with padded floors and walls, and bars on the window so nobody could escape.

It was extremely rare that anyone escaped from this hospital. It seemed like a maximum security prison.

Eventually, I got out of solitary, but not for long. The second week, when they told me it was lunch time and that I needed to eat, I told them I wasn't hungry. One male staff member grabbed me by the hand. "Let's go," he said.

I was sick of them trying to control every little thing in my life. The schedule said I was supposed to eat, but I just wasn't hungry. What was the big deal about me not being hungry? "No! Get your stinking hand off me, man!" I swung my arm to break away from him.

He called another staff member over, and they both grabbed me. I was able to break away from them. Then several more staff came over. I counted six altogether. They lifted me up and carried me to solitary confinement.

Even with six guys they could barely control me. I was cussing and twisting and pulling and doing all I could to get away. By the time they got me to the room, they weren't satisfied with just tossing me in and locking the door. Instead, they put me on a bed so they could strap me down. I'm surprised they didn't give me a lobotomy. After all, it was still the '70s. When they had me strapped down, I was still squirming and cussing them out, so they swabbed my arm and shot me up with tranquilizers.

I was pissed off at all of them, pissed off at my mother for putting me here, pissed off at the world for dealing me such a shitty hand. This went on at least another eight or nine times. It became a game to me to see how many it would take to drag Robert off and calm him down. They got to know me quite well. Or they thought they did. In all, I was in the hospital three different times. This first time was about six months.

Anyway, the so-called doctor that was treating me came to me one day. "Robert, we need your help," he said. "You see little Johnny over there?"

"Yeah," I said.

"Well, he's not eating, and he's not very happy. I want you to look after him and do what you can to make sure he eats."

"What? I don't want to take care of him. You take care of him."

"Well we tried, but he's not responding to our treatment. He needs someone to talk to him and watch over him. Someone who's here all the time. Someone he could trust and have a relationship with. A friend."

A friend, I thought. I don't have any friends. I shrugged. "Okay."

I looked after the kid for a while. He started eating, and he seemed to take a liking to me. I did what the doc wanted me to do, which I later figured out was to get the focus off myself and start thinking of other people. Anyway, it wasn't long before the kid got tired of me and then someone else was asked to take care of him before he was discharged. I don't know who it was more beneficial for, the kid or me.

Even in a nuthouse, you can meet some really nice people. Based on what I'd seen in *One Flew over the Cuckoo's Nest*, I half expected a bunch of adults, but there were a lot of kids my age.

I met a girl, Marissa, while I was in there, and we became good friends. She was a pretty blonde with a pale complexion. Supposedly she was there because she was hanging around with some bad friends and got dragged into some pretty negative behavior by them. After seeing me being strapped down and hauled away several times by a half dozen men, she asked me why I got so angry all the time. I said I didn't like those people telling me what to do or touching me. After a couple of months of being in there, I told Marissa I'd had enough and that I had to get out of there. I was making a plan to escape, and I asked if she wanted to come with me. She agreed.

I started explaining my plan to her. "In a couple of days," I said, "they will take us out in the yard again. At that time we'll get Ray to create a diversion to distract the staff. I'll reach back once I'm on top of the wall, then grab you and help you over. Can you pull yourself up over the wall?"

"Yes," she said.

"Are you positive?"

"Yes."

"Okay, remember, when Ray distracts the staff, stay by me. That's our cue. That's when we'll go over. I'm only going to get one chance. If I get caught, I'll never see the outside again. You're positive you can make it over, right?"

"Yes."

"Late afternoon Wednesday, we are going out to the courtyard. Stay by me."

At the chosen time, Ray started throwing rocks over the fence. The staff gathered round him and told him to stop. Then they grabbed him, and Ray started to make a big scene.

I whispered to Marissa, "Let's go."

I dragged a table and chair over to the fence. After several tries, I was able to leap and grab the top of the wall and pull myself up.

Then I turned around when I got to the top, with my body mostly dangling on the outside of the fence, my torso balancing on top of the fence. I yelled to Marissa, "Come on now. Jump and grab my hand. Let's go."

She tried leaping and clawing at the wall, but she was just short of reaching my hand.

I said, "C'mon, climb. Jump. Grab my hand."

I noticed the staff now looking at us. They were getting off of Ray and were running over to us.

"C'mon, Marissa, jump. You can make it. Grab my hand."

She cried, "I can't. Just go without me. Go, Rob. They're coming!"

"C'mon, you can do this," I said. "We're getting out of here together."

"Nooo!" she said. "I can't. Just go!"

With the staff coming closer and closer, I looked at her. "Are you sure?"

"Yeah, just go without me," she cried.

I jumped down on the outside just as they were about to grab my hand. I started running like I never ran before. I heard the alarm sound and realized it would only be a few moments before the security guard would be in the car looking for me. And the police too.

This wasn't a good neighborhood, and it was getting dark, so I just kept running. I made my way down a few streets, past barking dogs and random bits of conversation coming from cars and doorways. I was breathing heavily as I tried to keep running as fast as I could. I changed my direction several times, zigzagging through the neighborhood but still heading in the direction where I thought the highway was going to be. Eventually I heard the sound of speeding cars and knew I was close.

I finally made it to the highway. I stopped, gasping for air. It was hot and humid out, and I was covered in sweat. I got on the highway ramp, stuck my thumb out, and got picked up right away. I could not have planned that any better. I kept thinking of Marissa, who I'd left behind. I hoped she'd be okay, as well as Ray, who'd provided the distraction. I hoped Marissa understood I did everything I could to try and bring her with me.

"Where you going?" the driver asked.

"Palatine. I'm going home."

Three rides and a several hours later, I made it home. My mom was there, and she wasn't that surprised to see me. She'd been notified of my escape. She agreed, for at least the time being, to not take me back there.

I went to my room and lay on the bed and just stared up at the ceiling, thinking about what I'd just been through. Most of it was bullshit as far as I was concerned, but there were a couple of positive things. Meeting Marissa was cool. And there was one staff member who really blew me away. I found myself dwelling on one of the experiences I had with him. In addition to working at the hospital, he was also an artist. He'd drawn the album cover for Earth Wind & Fire's latest album. Without me knowing it, while we were playing a board game with the group, he made a pencil drawing of me.

"Here," he said, handing it to me. "What do you think?"

I took the paper and looked at it. I couldn't believe what I was looking at. I was stunned. "Is this me? Are you sure?"

"Yes, that's you"

The sketch I was looking at shook me. I felt ugly, dark, and evil. This was a sketch of a handsome young man. Why hadn't I ever been able to see this person before? Why hadn't I been able to see the beauty in this person? I took the picture back to my room in the hospital and stared at it. I couldn't take my eyes off it. I looked at every line, trying to understand how he'd seen that image behind the monster I felt myself to be. I couldn't sleep that night and stared at the drawing well into the early morning hours, breaking down in tears several times. That picture shook me to my core. I struggled to reconcile the monster I felt myself to be with the handsome young man the artist had somehow seen in me.

Eventually, Marissa did get out of the hospital, but the right way. She was discharged. She called to let me know she was out, and we made plans to go to a concert. I was excited because she was a seriously cute girl. Also, because we'd both been in the hospital, I felt like she knew me in ways that other girls didn't. Or at least I didn't have to feel like I had to hide stuff from her or explain things about myself.

The concert was Blue Oyster Cult, and we went in a group—Marissa, a couple of her friends, and me. On the way there, we each had a couple of beers. As we walked in, Marissa seemed kind of out of it. She bumped into me a few times. I wouldn't have minded that, but she just didn't seem herself. I hadn't realized how heavily a couple of beers would affect her.

"Are you feeling okay?" I said. A huge crowd was swirling all around us, and I had to raise my voice a little to be heard.

She smiled a little too big. "I feel just fine," she said. "But I do have to use the bathroom."

"Now?" I said. I looked from her to the inner doors of the concert hall and back to her. "It's about to start."

"I won't be long," she said, and she tottered off to the ladies room.

Her friends hung out with me. We all wanted to sit together. Marissa was in there five minutes, then ten minutes. Finally I asked her girl-friend to go check on her, but before she could do that, Marissa came out of the bathroom, stumbled toward us, then just collapsed on the floor. Her wonderful friends ran into the interior of the hall, leaving me there with her.

I knew right away she was overdosing on drugs. I had no idea what she'd taken. All I'd had was the beer, and whatever she and her friends had, they didn't share with me. It took the paramedics a few minutes to revive her. Then they made many attempts to find her vein so they could give her something in an IV. It didn't go well. Blood was shooting everywhere. It was a surreal scene. Some people were just standing around watching, which I thought was out of line, but then others were just walking past like there was nothing special going on, and that was disturbing too.

Finally the paramedics were able to get the needle in her arm. Once they had her relatively stabilized, they put her on a gurney and wheeled her out to an ambulance. It wasn't until a week or so later that I was able to find out that she was okay.

At the time, I thought I'd done a pretty good job of shrugging off the whole thing, but in the years to come, I developed a serious anxiety about going out to events or about anything out of the ordinary that came up. It took me years to put two and two together and realize that my anxiety might have had something to do with that incident.

Of course, that wasn't the first time I'd experienced trauma associated with going to a special event. On the day my mother tried to murder my sisters and me, she'd said she was taking us to the Ice Capades. That incident in my childhood, coupled with the OD at the concert in my teen years, really seemed to do a number on me emotionally.

If I had to go out to some event that was supposed to be fun, I'd end up feeling very uneasy, as if I were in some kind of danger and something bad was going to happen to me. I didn't understand it at the time, but now I know it was something that was programmed into my subconscious by my mom's actions. It was years before I overcame it.

CHAPTER **14**

DAD AND LIES

L ike most boys, I wanted to think my dad was all-knowing and fair. You don't understand what parents go through until you become one. In some ways, Dad was a lot more understanding than Mom.

One Saturday morning, I wanted to run to the store real quick and pick up some milk. I slid in behind the wheel of my dad's yellow Pontiac LeMans and tried to start it, but the battery was dead. I didn't know much about cars, but I wanted to jump start it with the other car to help out. It turned out I crossed the cables and fried the alternator. When I realized what I'd done, I cursed the car, went back inside, and flopped down on the couch to watch TV.

A half hour later Dad strolled through the room and out the front door. I called out softly after him, not really wanting him to turn around, not really wanting to tell him what I'd done.

The next minute he was back inside. "What happened to the car?" he said. "It's not starting at all."

I sat up on the couch and rubbed my hands together, ready for some drama. "Uh, okay, the battery was dead, so I tried jumping it, but it didn't seem to work."

He went back out to look at the car. When he came back in he said, "You know why you couldn't jump start it?"

Here we go, I thought. Here comes the yelling. "Uh, I'm not sure."

"Well, it looks to me like you probably got the cables crossed. It's black to black and red to red. Do you understand that now?"

"Yeah, I do now."

He shrugged his shoulders. "Now you know how to jump start a car." Then he went in the kitchen to call somebody for a ride.

I looked over my shoulder at him as he left the room, my mouth open. There was no yelling, no screaming, just a simple life lesson taught to a son by his father.

These were the times I noticed a major difference between my dad and my mom. At least Dad was more understanding—when he wasn't drinking. But I came to understand that even if we have a good side—good qualities—if we don't share them and try to aspire to become better people, we become what we share most of the time.

Eventually my dad bought a car for me. Well, it was a project car. It was a 1972 Ford Maverick. Maybe he was trying to say something about my personality. Supposedly it was a sports car, but it was that in name only. The car was only a few years old, but it was already rusted through on both of the rear quarter panels. It needed bodywork and a new paint job in the worst way. He said we'd work on it together, and then it would be my car. I thought that was great. My own car. No more walking or bumming rides.

We worked on it in the evenings and on the weekends. It was a good project for us. Not only was I going to end up with a car, but it gave us some father and son time. Maybe that was my dad's intention all along—to do something practical that would keep me out of trouble at the same time.

I always seemed to be getting into some kind of trouble. Most of the time it was my fault, but there were other times when trouble just seemed to follow me. Wherever I was, it found me. We worked on the car for about a month or so. He even let me pick out the color of the paint. I chose a medium metallic blue that sparkled in the sunlight. It was definitely a cool color. I was proud of that car. We had set out to get it in shape, and we accomplished that goal together. Now it was all mine.

So I thought.

I felt betrayed again. My dad, who I thought was great to give me a car, took it back. As we were putting on the finishing touches, we'd begun to fight again. By the time we finished the car, I told him I was going back to live with Mom.

"Just give me the keys, and I'll get out of here," I said.

My dad shook his head and crossed his arms. "The car stays."

"You told me this car was mine," I yelled.

"The car stays," he said again.

You bastard, I thought. I stormed into the house, packed a few things, and took off on foot. After all that time and effort we put in to fixing up that car, Dad ended up selling it.

I stayed at Mom's place for a while, but my life wasn't any better there, and a few months later, I ended up moving back to my Dad's place again.

All the chaos in my life was affecting my schoolwork. It wasn't unusual for me to get some static from my teachers. One of them was just out of college and only a few years older than me. She was an attractive, petite brunette—only about five feet tall.

One day after class, she asked me to stay behind for a minute. I thought she was going to talk to me about my homework or something, but after all the other students had left the room, she asked me if I liked Todd Rundgren.

"He's okay," I said. "Why do you ask?"

"He's going to be in town next weekend. Do you want to go with me?"

I had no idea what was going on. It almost seemed like she was asking me out on a date, but she was my high school teacher. Maybe she was just trying to be nice to me, to mentor me. But I was so unsure of myself and of the situation that I didn't go with her. Maybe it was totally innocent on her part. But by that time I'd seen plenty that wasn't.

I had a hard time functioning in school. My grades were poor. I was in special ed because I couldn't concentrate. After I had moved back to my dad's again, he promised me if I would make the honor roll, he would send me to college. I worked very hard in school, and with the help of many of my teachers I was able to make the honor roll the last semester of my junior year.

After I got my report card, I was so proud of myself. Coming through all the problems I'd had, I felt I'd accomplished something great. It had taken a lot of focus and hard work. That was the first time I'd really had a goal to work toward. So to be able to keep it in front of me and stay focused felt great. I couldn't wait to tell my dad. I knew he was going to be proud of me. And I knew college would be great.

When I got home, I ran into the house waving the report card and yelling the good news.

He looked up at me from the couch with a faint smile on his face, seeming a little distracted. "Good job," he said, and then he went back to watching TV. He obviously didn't appreciate all the hard work I'd put into my schoolwork or what it meant to me.

But I was still excited. "Now I can go to college," I said. "I'm so excited!"

He looked up at me again, puzzled instead of smiling. "What do you mean?"

"You told me at the beginning of the semester that you'd send me to college if I made the honor roll this semester."

"I never said that."

"What? Oh, yes you did! You promised."

He shook his head. "I don't remember saying that. I'm not sending you to college."

"You liar!" I yelled.

He ignored me. To me, he was just another person who didn't do what they said they would. The world was not to be trusted. I couldn't trust him to even care about his own son. Even when I ran away, he didn't seem to care. And he never discussed it with me or asked if I was okay after it happened. Did he not love me and care about me? Today, looking back I have to think he did, but he didn't know how to express it.

CHAPTER **15**

IT JUST
TAKES ONE

A few days after Dad told me he wasn't sending me to college, my stepmom came home from work and found him half in the bag.

Dad came into my room out of the blue and started yelling at me. He said he was tired of me and my smart mouth.

I had no idea where this attitude was coming from. I hadn't done anything to provoke him, and I just wanted to be left alone. I stood up because I felt vulnerable sitting on my bed. "What are you talking about?" I said.

He pushed me, and I fell backward and braced myself with one arm on the bed to keep myself upright. "C'mon," he said. "Let's go. You want to fight me? You think you're a tough guy?"

I straightened up again and sidestepped him. "I don't know what you're talking about."

He pushed me harder this time. I lost my balance and fell to the floor.

He stood over me. "C'mon, let's go. You want to fight me, let's go right now."

"No," I yelled, scrambling to my feet. "I'm not going to fight you!"

Just like that, his anger left him, and he appeared calm. "Okay, let's go out on the patio and have a beer together."

"What?"

He moved toward the door and waved me forward. "Let's go out on the patio and have a beer."

"I'm not going to have a beer with you."

He stumbled out of my room by himself. I closed the door and laid down on my bed again. What the hell was that man thinking? I was just minding my own business and out of know where .... Where did that come from? Was it me? I didn't understand that men like my dad had issues that had nothing to do with me. I just saw myself as the problem.

Talk about a ping pong ball. I bounced from one parent to another. I must have moved something like eighteen times up to that point. I really couldn't get along with either of them. I ended up living back at my mom's house again. All this moving was starting to wear on me, but after the confrontation with my dad, I didn't want anything more to do with him.

About the middle of the first semester of my senior year, my guidance counselor told me that due to all the time I'd missed in school, I didn't have enough credits to graduate with the rest of my class. So I would have to stay back a year. I told her there was no way I was going to school for another year.

That was it for me. As soon as I got out of the office, I walked right out the front door and dropped out of school that day.

After spending a few months bouncing from one menial job to another, I thought college might be a better alternative, even if I did have to pay for it myself. First, of course, I'd have to get a GED. I decided to ask for guidance from one of the teachers who'd really taken the time to make sure I was learning and who'd helped me make the honor roll during my junior year. I figured she'd point me in the right direction.

She told me she wanted to help. She gave me directions to her home and told me to come over to study after she was done with school for the day. She seemed sincere. I was extremely grateful to her. For the first time I could remember, I had a sense of deep appreciation and gratitude for someone. She helped me over several nights preparing for the GED test. I took it a few days later, and thanks to her, I passed. This was one of the very few times I truly felt someone cared about me. I've always been grateful for what she did for me.

CHAPTER **16**

ADRENALINE AND BAD DECISIONS

I seemed to get along with girls pretty easily, and I always had more female friends than male friends. I don't know if it was because I was better looking than a lot of other guys or if I was less threatening. I wasn't aggressive, and I think girls appreciated that. Deb was a girl I knew from high school. I always wanted to go out with her, but she never seemed interested in me in that way. We weren't compatible as a couple, but we became good friends. Lisa was another high school friend who hung out with Deb and me. I was strictly platonic with both of them.

One day the three of us were at Deb's house. She was reading *Cosmo* and came upon an item about a contest they were having. The idea was for a girl to take some sexy photos of her guy and send them in for a chance to win a weekend getaway. So Lisa and Deb came up with this idea to take pictures of me in bed with a sheet covering very little of me. They explained to me how they were going to do it and what kind of poses they wanted me to do.

"Robert, with your body and long hair, these photos would be very hot and sexy," said Deb. "We might have a pretty good chance to win!"

I rolled my eyes. "C'mon, guys. We're not going to win."

"Yeah, but think about how much fun it would be," said Lisa. "Come on, Robert. Let's do it!"

Although it would have been fun, I felt vulnerable. It wasn't so much about the racy pictures as it was more about my lack of self-esteem. Looking back, I realize I should have done it, but at the time I didn't feel that good about myself and certainly not as sexy as they were making me out to be. Exposing myself would mean I would be open to criticism, and even though I got along well with these two girls, I couldn't take any criticism from them or anyone else. Even compliments were hard to take after having been pushed down so much. I didn't feel worthy of praise, and I even doubted the sincerity of anyone who tried to compliment me.

In May of 1979, shortly after I got my GED, I started a job as a car porter at Bill Cook Buick, in Arlington Heights. I thought I would start saving for college.

One of the other porters that worked at the dealership was always a little sarcastic to me, and he was kind of a bully to the other porters and detail guys. He was bigger than I was. Maybe because he'd been there so long, he seemed to think everybody should bow down to him. He always threw his weight around. He started getting on my nerves to the point where I wasn't going to put up with him anymore. One day I told him to shut his mouth, and when he didn't we started going at it. He got in a few good shots, but so did I. And after we were done, he never smarted off to me or the other kids again.

I still didn't have any transportation of my own. I sometimes drove my mom's car, but I couldn't always use it when I needed it, so I had to get something. One of the guys who worked in the body shop had an awesome looking motorcycle. I fell in love with it the moment I saw it. It was a Kawasaki 900 Z1 with a red and orange gas tank, a king and queen seat, ape hanger handle bars, and an eight-inch extension on the front end that made it look like a small chopper. I loved that bike, and even though I'd never ridden a motorcycle before, I asked him if he wanted to sell it.

"For fifteen hundred bucks I'd sell it," he said.

Well, I didn't have that much money. So I started looking for something else, and I decided it really should be a car.

I gave an elderly lady a ride home one day, and she ended up selling me her silver-beige 1968 Olds 442. It had low miles, but it needed a little bodywork on the quarter panels. If you would just tap the gas, it would burn rubber. The car's power was more than I could handle, but I always drove it fast, loving the power that I had at my fingertips.

One Saturday, a couple of my friends wanted to get together and go out with some girls they'd met in a neighboring town.

"Sure, I'm game," I said. "Let's get some beer, and I'll pick you up around eight and we'll head out."

We were already a little tipsy when we arrived at the house of one of the girls. She had her two friends over, and we hung around and talked to them for a while. We asked them to go for a ride, and they said no. Considering what lay ahead for us, that was probably the smartest decision those girls had made in their lives up to that moment.

Not more than a couple of minutes after we left the girls, I was driving faster than I should have been, and I took a curve too fast. Before I could begin to slow down, a driver pulled right out in front of me. I whipped the wheel hard to the right, but I clipped the other car then jumped the curb and was knocked unconscious. One of the guys in the car was thrown out the back window and suffered severe head injuries. The girl who pulled out in front of me got her arm broken from being spun around and slammed into the door. But I didn't know any of this. I was out cold.

I had no idea where I was. I was flat on my back, looking up at a fluorescent light surrounded by ceiling tiles. As I tried to expand my attention to my surroundings, I realized there were tubes sticking out of my body. I could hear the whir of machines. The light hurt my eyes, and every time

I took a breath, I felt a sharp pain in my ribs. When I tried to shift my position, my abdomen hurt.

"Robert, you're awake," said a woman in a calm voice.

I managed to turn my head a little in the direction of her voice and saw that she was wearing a nurse's uniform.

"Don't try to move too much," she said. "Do you know where you are?"

"Hospital?"

"Right. You're in intensive care. You've had some internal injuries and internal bleeding, but we're taking good care of you."

"Internal injuries from what?" I said.

"You were in a car wreck. Do you not remember?"

I hadn't, but I did then. I'd been at the wheel of my '68 Olds 442. "Oh God," I said.

"Apparently you were moving pretty fast when it happened. You're lucky."

"Lucky I was moving fast?"

"Lucky to be alive."

I sure as hell didn't feel lucky. And then I remembered the other guy who'd been in the car with me. He hadn't been lucky either. I'd just met him the day before and we'd decided to hang out. I was sure he wished we hadn't. "Hey, what about my friend?"

"He's going to be okay. He's pretty beat up. Like you."

I felt terrible about having hurt him. I didn't even want to stay around. I was afraid he would hate me or kill me when he got better. I didn't want to see him anymore.

I made a feeble attempt to sit up.

"Take it easy," said the nurse, gently pushing me back down on the bed.

"I'm just gonna go," I said.

"Doubt it. You just woke up from being unconscious due to a bad car wreck. You're not going anywhere. The doctor will be in soon to speak with you, and he'll tell you when you might get out of here, but it won't be today. Okay?"

The pain from trying to sit up was coursing through my body. "Yeah, I guess you're right."

"Always. Remember that," she said, and she breezed out of the room.

I manage to turn my head enough to see that there was a phone on the nightstand next to me. Moving very slowly, I was able to navigate through the pain until my hand had reached the phone. I punched up the number of my friend Ricky. Ricky was a little squirrely guy. I liked him because he loved cars and loved to party. Also, he had a Kawasaki, and we used to ride together. Of all my party friends, he was the one I felt I could trust the most. I knew he came from a good family. And I saw just from hanging around with him that he had a good heart and a good work ethic. Of course, he did end up doing six months in jail on a drug charge, but that was my circle at the time.

"Ricky," I said into the phone. "This is Rob, man. I'm in the hospital."

"What?" he said. "What the hell happened?"

"I was just in a bad wreck, man. Can you stop by my house and get me some clothes, then come pick me up? I'm getting out of here."

He showed up a couple hours later with some clothes and a shocked look on his face. He looked at all the tubes sticking out of me and stopped dead in his tracks. "Woah, Rob, are you sure you should be leaving?"

"It's worse than it looks," I said. And then I laughed. "I mean it looks worse than it is. They got me doped up." I sat up and pulled the tubes out of my arms. "See, that looks better, right?"

He raised his eyebrows and cocked his head. "Whatever you say, man."

I got out of my hospital gown and pulled my clothes on. Then we snuck out of there quietly and quickly. Later on I found out the other guy, who had a severe head injury, was fine and started working for a local police department. I heard he was not mad at me, but that didn't make me feel any better.

My Olds was history. When it came to dealing with people and things, my habitual irresponsibility always seemed to screw things up for me. And the thing with the car wreck was a major example of that. Part of my recklessness was due to the fact that I felt invincible, untouchable. Or maybe I just didn't care what touched me. I think that buried deep inside me was the fact that I didn't care whether I lived or died. But obviously there were other people involved. It was bad enough that I wasn't handling my own life responsibly; my behavior was having an impact on other people too. I never hurt anybody intentionally, but that didn't make it any less terrible. People were suffering because of me.

CHAPTER **17**

CAROL

I had a knack for meeting girls. A few months after my accident, in June of 1980, I went to a party with my younger sister. I was introduced to a girl by Sherri, a friend of my sister. Sherri introduced me to her friend Carol. I was very attracted to Carol, and I felt she was also attracted to me as well. She was very cute. She was a couple of years younger than me, about five-foot six and 115 pounds. She had a pleasant personality, wavy strawberry-blonde hair, beautiful curves, a body to die for.

She was quiet, so at first I couldn't really get a sense of what she was thinking, but she laughed at my jokes and didn't want to run away from me, so that was something. We became friends and went on a casual date. She was a waitress at Perkins and lived with her mom in a small townhome about a twelve-minute walk from my mom's house in Palatine. She never really talked about her dad, but she'd kept his last name. Her mom had remarried and divorced again.

Sherri, the girl who'd introduced us at the party, heard that we went out, and for some reason she got it into her head that she wanted to go out with me too. Sherri called me and asked me if I wanted to go out with her. Carol and I had only been on one date, and it wasn't even anything serious, so I thought it couldn't hurt to just go out with Sherri, since I wasn't really serious about her either, so I said yes.

After our date, she said she wanted to show me her place. It was actually her mom's place, but her mom was never home. When we got there, she asked me to come upstairs.

The next time Carol and I went out, again, we were just hanging out. Nothing serious. We sat down at dinner, and after the waitress took our order, Carol looked at me.

"Have you been out on a date with Sherri?"

The question caught me off guard. I didn't see what the big deal was, but I blushed a little. "Yes."

"Why did you go out with her?"

"Carol, you didn't seem that interested in me, and we only went out once."

She sighed and looked at me, eyebrows arched. "Robert, I like you. Don't you know that she did that to get back at me?"

"Why? What did you do to her?"

"Nothing, but she thought that I intentionally went out with someone she was interested in."

I genuinely felt bad. "I'm sorry, Carol. I didn't mean to hurt you. That's the last thing I want to do."

Carol seemed to be a bit different than most girls I met. It didn't take long before our thoughts were in sync, and we could read each other almost perfectly. Not only that, it was like she was clairvoyant. She seemed to sense what I was thinking. Sometimes she even knew what I was about to say. So we really felt comfortable and were happy around each other.

Early in our relationship, we had to overcome one major obstacle. A couple months before I met her, I'd made plans to go to college in order to try and make a better life for myself. I planned to leave in the fall. That became an issue.

Before I went away, I spent a lot of time working. I was making decent money and saving to get something I wanted. I went back to the old dealership I worked at to visit Eric, the guy with the Kawasaki Z1 900. I was totally in love with that bike and worked my ass off with it in mind.

"Hey, Eric, guess what?" I said when I walked into the shop.

"Hey, Rob. Long time. What's up?"

I handed him a fat white envelope, grinning like a maniac.

He opened it and pulled out a stack of cash. He counted it in disbelief.

"That's how much you said you'd sell the bike for, right?"

He chuckled and pulled the keys from his pocket. "It's yours, man."

I took the keys with my heart pumping adrenaline. I was overjoyed, but the truth was I'd never ridden a motorcycle before. I was wondering how I was going to get this thing home. A Kawasaki Z1 900 is a huge beast.

I climbed on and looked at Eric. "How do I shift?"

"It's one down and four up. Just pull in the clutch, on the left handle bar, and then push down or lift up on the gear shift. Nothing to it."

I nodded, still smiling. "Okay," I said. I started the engine and rode away.

I wouldn't say there was nothing to it. First of all, sitting on top of this monster, I felt like I was doing the splits. The seat was wide and sitting right above the powerful engine. It felt like I was actually riding a rocket. The whole way home I was amazed that I was actually riding it, and I was just hoping I'd get there without completely screwing up.

When I got to my place, I parked the bike on the sidewalk out front, got off, and just stared at it for a while, trying to convince myself that it was really mine. It seemed insane that I owned it and that I'd ridden it all the way home. I'd never been on anything with that much power or speed before, let alone with two wheels.

I got a lot more comfortable riding it. I also got *very* comfortable with the looks I got from everyone when I rode. I'd be at a stoplight and somebody would roll down their windows and say, "Hey, nice bike!" The more I drove it, the more relaxed and confident I felt. It was a great bike. I loved the openness, the way it made me feel free, the wind blowing through my hair. And I felt I had real power in my hands. Carol also liked my new bike, and we would take long day trips on it up north in the country.

I made some of the best friends in my life at my job at Republic Lumber—a hardware and lumber store. These were the kinds of friends I wasn't use to. The "friends" I knew before used people and did anything they could to profit at the expense of others. My new friends were honest, caring, and spoke kindly of others. Based on my experience, I always thought those friends only existed on TV or in the movies. I wasn't used to being around people like that. I felt I was out of my environment, but for some reason I couldn't figure, people started looking up to me at work. I worked in shipping and receiving and went out on the floor often to restock, and to help out when I could. I'd never been somebody others looked up to. The way they looked at me made me start to look at myself a little differently. I never mentioned anything about my past, my home life, or the time I ran away. All these kids at work were well-off, seemed to have good families, and were all getting their college paid for by their parents. I started to wonder what my life would have been like if I'd had a good family life.

One of my coworkers was a guy named Tom, a spunky Navy guy in his sixties. I told him I was training for an organized fight called Battle of the Brawlers. This type of fighting was unheard of in the '70s. He told me he used to be the boxing champ of his ship. I thought that was awesome. He gave me some pointers on fighting.

I took his advice and added it to my training regimen. I was not that great a fighter, but I was an angry kid, and I felt I always had something to prove. One month before the fight, the city of Chicago got a court injunction to stop the promoters from holding it. They claimed it was too barbaric.

CHAPTER **18**

BOB

After my fight was canceled, I started to be more involved at the store and with my coworkers. Back when I was in high school, I used to get together with guys in the park, and we played a variation of softball. It was played with a sixteen-inch ball without gloves. I organized a softball team among the workers in the store. It was a great time. We played other stores that had organized softball teams, too. Carol would often come and watch us play. Looking back, I see that these were some of the best times of my life.

Playing softball strengthened some of my friendships with the guys at Republic Lumber. One of these guys was Bob. He was my best friend there, and we hung out a lot outside of work.

One day, Bob asked me if I wanted to go to a concert up in Wisconsin, at Alpine Valley. He told me Journey was playing. Journey was one of my favorite bands at the time, and I jumped at the chance to see them. We decided to take his boat, a dark green Olds 98 convertible.

It was a beautiful summer day to be driving a convertible. We stopped on the way up to pick up some beverages. We each bought a fifth of vodka and some orange juice. It was an hour and a half drive, but it seemed to go pretty quick. By the time we got there, Bob had finished his bottle. I was still nursing mine but had a very good buzz going. By the time we took our lawn seats, we definitely felt no pain.

About halfway through the show, Bob told me he had to take a leak and ventured off. I continued to enjoy the show, singing along to my favorite songs, just riding the feeling. But I was alone. Journey finished the concert and came back for their encore. I loved it, but there was nobody to share it with. Bob still hadn't gotten back. They did an encore of about five songs. When they left the stage for good, still no Bob. Now I was getting a little concerned. People were pouring out of the lawn area and were heading home. I watched the place pretty much empty out, and I kept asking the people who passed me if they'd seen my friend. Nope. Nobody had a clue where he was.

It was a little more than an hour before the place had cleared out completely. There was one remaining staff person who saw me still looking for Bob. He came back into the stadium. "Are you looking for someone?" he asked.

"Yeah!"

He nodded knowingly. "Follow me."

With him in the lead, we made our way out to the parking lot. The huge field of asphalt was empty. Except for one car way out in the distance. The Olds 98 convertible.

"Is this the guy you're looking for?" said the staff member.

I peered into the distance, trying to see if anybody was in the car.

"Hey," said the guy. "Not out there. Right here."

I turned to where he was pointing. Bob was leaning up against a post by the entrance of the parking lot, passed out.

"Holy jeez," I said. "Yeah, that's him. Thanks."

"No prob," said the guy, and he turned and walked back into the stadium.

I walked over to Bob and called his name. He didn't move. I grabbed his shoulder and shook him. His head wagged back and forth, but he still didn't respond. I checked to see if he was breathing, and he was. So I tried to pick him up. Bob was a little bigger than I was—about two hundred pounds. Eventually we made it to the car, so this meant I had to drive this boat home, and I had no idea how to get there. Besides, I may have been a lot better off than Bob, but there was no way I was in any shape to drive. I just pointed the car the way I thought we were supposed to go and started driving.

I was driving for at least an hour before I even recognized any landmarks. I was trying to blink the vodka away as I struggled to keep the car between the lines. The cool morning air helped keep me awake, and at about two in the morning we got back to my house. It was one long ride home. Bob spent the night at my place.

We went into work together the next morning, but Bob wasn't in good shape. He worked in shipping and receiving and would sometimes go out on the floor to stock. Not that day. He didn't venture out onto the floor at all, and he spent a lot of time in the bathroom. It was a slow day anyway, and one of the two assistant managers, who knew where we'd gone the night before, told Bob to go home. "You're no use to me today," he said, patting him on the back.

CHAPTER **19**

BROKEN
PROMISES

Life seemed to be looking up. The time came for me to leave for college. I had been accepted into Western New Mexico University, but I decided to switch to a school in Hawaii. Besides the better weather and being in the tropics, the counselor at the university told me they had a football program and said she could help find me work. And besides all that, the farther I could get away from home the better. New Mexico was far; Hawaii was farther. Actually, with my dad, it didn't matter how far apart we were. We still argued.

I was getting ready to leave for Hawaii and needed to say goodbye to Carol. I knew that was going to be hard. She was a quiet person but very loving and caring. She kept to herself a lot, so I had become the center of her social life. She came over to my place the day before I left, and we went to my room. She was visibly upset that I was leaving.

I put my arms around her. "This is for the best," I said "I'll miss you. You're a great girl. Look, we'll write and stay in touch, okay?"

I broke my embrace and looked into her face as I held her shoulders.

"Okay, I know."

I could see she was struggling to hold back the tears. I felt bad, but this was something I had to do.

I left for Hawaii with my all stuff, not even thinking about the fact that I'd have no place to live when I got there. My counselor said she would help me find a job, which was good because I could start working right away. I only had enough money for a few months. After I found a place to live, I could start focusing on trying out for football.

When I landed on the Big Island, I was blown away. It was just as stunning as it is on postcards. Between the gate and the main part of the terminal, everything was open to the outside, not enclosed like other airports I'd seen. I saw Mauna Kea for the first time from the airport. It was snowcapped. In August! I was walking from the airport to the hotel, and right on the street a local asked me if I wanted to buy some pakalolo.

I laughed. I thought he was pulling my leg, speaking some kind of Pidgin for the dumb tourist. "Some what?" I said.

"Pakalolo, man. Marijuana."

"Really? That's what it's called here?"

He smiled and nodded enthusiastically.

"Okay, that's cool, but no thanks, man."

He shrugged and wandered off.

The hotel room was touristy. There were paintings of Hawaiians paddling outrigger canoes and hula girls dancing, and the bedspread had a tropical floral design. After I got settled in, I decided go down to the bar and have a drink and relax a bit. The people were extremely friendly, especially one of the cocktail servers. She started hitting on me almost the moment I sat down. Being new in town and having a girlfriend, I wasn't interested. A few moments later her boyfriend came to visit her. He could barely make it through the doorway. He was the size of a sumo wrestler, carrying some fat but also plenty of muscle. He wasn't somebody I was going to fight with over a girl.

I found a place to live right away fairly close to school. It was in the mountains overlooking Hilo Bay. The owner rented some rooms and the basement out to some locals and college kids. There were seven others living in the house, including a divorced woman and her three children.

I decided to go to the university and get registered and to see my counselor. Her office was small and functional, but it did have a window, and as I was learning, anyplace on the island of Hawaii with a window was beautiful. We shook hands, and she offered me a seat across from her desk and leaned back, relaxing into the environment.

"So, not to seem too eager," I said, "but when do football tryouts start?"

She shook her head, bewildered. "We don't have football at this school."

I sat bolt upright, eyebrows raised. "Huh?"

"The football team plays on Oahu, at the main campus, University of Hawaii at Manoa, not here."

"You told me you had football on the campus on the Big Island when I spoke to you on the phone. That's one of the reasons I came to this school."

"I'm sorry, but you must have misunderstood me. We only have football at the main campus, on Oahu."

I was stunned and a little angry. I was sure she'd conned me, intentionally misleading me about the football program just to get me to go to her school. But there was nothing I could do about it. I slumped in my chair, not relaxed at all.

"Okay, so can you help me find a job like you said on the phone?"

She smiled. "Let's get you settled first, then I'll see what I can do about helping you get a job."

I didn't like the sound of that. She'd promised football and help with a job. Not getting to play football was a huge bummer, but I could live with that. Not getting a job was a much bigger deal. I only had enough money to last me a couple months. If I couldn't make more, my college days would end rather abruptly.

After the first few days of classes, I checked back with my counselor about the job she'd promised to find me. I was sitting in the same chair, the same beautiful view out the window.

"Robert, I tried, but I'm sorry," she said. "I wasn't able to find you anything."

Again, I sat up in the chair. "What? You're kidding, right? You told me on the phone when I was still in Illinois that you could find me a job. I trusted you to be able to do that for me. Now you are telling me you can't? No job, no football. Thanks a lot." I practically leapt out of the chair and flew out the door.

I stomped across the beautiful campus in a foul mood. Not even a job at the university. That was bad, because I knew there were not many jobs around town. I was really relying on my counselor to pull through for me. Apparently, I relied too much on her. Even when things seemed to be looking up they ended up going straight down.

Even a tropical paradise like Hawaii is nothing without money. Well, almost nothing. Three months later with no job and no money the only thing I could do was go home. I didn't want to call my mother, so I called someone I could count on—Carol. I don't know how she did it, but she got the money for a ticket and mailed it to me. I was on my way home after only a few months at school. I felt like a complete failure.

When I got back to Illinois, I went directly from the airport to Carol's school to surprise her. I ran into her in the smoking area. When she saw me walk in, she didn't seem that surprised to see me. She just took another drag on her cigarette.

I was a little heartbroken. "Are you not happy to see me?"

"Yes, I am."

Even though she sent me the ticket, she seemed tense. It was like she had a sense that something was wrong in my life—something off-kilter about my presence there. But I knew she'd relax around me again quickly.

I lived with a friend for a few months then went back to my mom's. Tension between us had eased, perhaps because I was older. Anyway, we were getting along better. It was April 1981. Carol and I had been dating for ten months, and I'd fallen deeply in love with her. She was the first person in my life who really showed me love and compassion and who was truly genuine and sincere toward me. I wanted to share my entire life with her. I knew this was the girl for me, and I know in my heart she wanted to spend the rest of her life with me too. We were inseparable. I decided I was going to ask her to marry me on her birthday, June 18. Even though it was difficult to wait because of my love and passion for her and my excitement about my plan to ask her to marry me, I just needed a little more time to be able to afford a nice engagement ring for her. I'd been out shopping for them. Or window shopping, at least. And anytime I was at a mall, I always wandered into the jewelry store, just to dream about getting her something nice.

What a feeling to be in love and to be loved. It regenerated my heart, soul, and my outlook on life.

CHAPTER 20

MYSTERIOUS
PAINFUL SACRIFICE

The drinking age in Wisconsin was only eighteen, and Carol was seventeen. She could pass for eighteen, so she frequently asked me if we could go up to Wisconsin to go drinking. But we never could seem to make it up there. Either I was working or she was or we had something to do with other friends.

On the afternoon of May 3, 1981 (not a date I could ever forget), Carol and I were having a good time just hanging out in my room, listening to albums, old and new, and just talking.

Then the phone rang. It was Bob. "Robert, do you and Carol want to go up to Wisconsin and do some drinking tonight?"

This was something that should have made me happy. But the question sent a chill down my spine. I was blown away by the feeling. It was a mystical experience. I heard the words he was saying, but it was almost like the words weren't the meaningful part of the conversation. I had a sense something terrible was going to happen, but I tried to block it out and focus on the rational. This was a good thing, a chance to take Carol drinking in Wisconsin like she always wanted. It made perfect rational sense. I turned to Carol to ask her if she wanted to go. The feelings of happiness we'd had a few moments earlier evaporated. I knew she wanted to go up there. And when we looked into each other's eyes, she knew what I was going to say before I said it.

I felt like we were communicating with our thoughts instead of words. Something ran through my body like I'd never felt before. I was like I was getting a mild shock with cold electricity.

We both recognized what was going to happen that night, and it wasn't good. We didn't say it to each other because we didn't need to. I felt with a commanding sense of intuition and profound humbleness that Carol knew this night was coming and that she realized it was her destiny. I'd never had that feeling before, and I've never had it since.

"Yes, we can go," she said. And she had a deep sadness in her eyes.

At that moment, a thought raced through my mind. I wanted so much to ask her to make love to me. One last time. Regretfully, I couldn't bring myself to say it.

Bob came over early that evening with another guy we worked with, a softball teammate named John. I didn't know John that well, but we all got along just fine. We piled into Bob's station wagon and headed up to Wisconsin a little earlier than we really had to so that we could leave for home a little earlier, before all the drunks hit the road. We took our time driving up and then stopped for dinner and had a great time. Since my childhood friend Timmy, I'd never had a good friend like Bob. He was a kind, gentle soul who always lent you a hand, whether you wanted one or not. These kinds of friends do not come along very often in one's life. The atmosphere of the family restaurant and the presence of good friends made it easy for me to put the mystical experience I'd had earlier out of my mind and just enjoy the "real world." Dinner with good friends made sense. But that mystical event had been a call from my higher self. I've come to understand that if you don't answer that call, your higher self hangs up, in a sense. And you can miss out on vitally important messages that way.

We arrived in Twin Lakes, Wisconsin, around seven that warm, May evening. We started drinking at one of the bars pretty much as soon as we arrived, and then we moved on to several others. We ended up at a bar with pool and foosball tables. We played several games of pool, breaking off into teams—Carol and I against Bob and John. I started off hot, but the more I drank, the more shots I missed. Of course, this was also true of everybody else, so we stayed pretty even. When we really started screwing up our shots, we decided it was getting a little late and we should probably get going before the bars closed and everyone started heading back to Illinois. We decided we'd all use the bathrooms and then meet back at the bar before we headed out to the car.

Several minutes later, everybody had gotten back to the bar except Carol. We were just making idle conversation when I realized she'd been gone too long. "Have any of you guys seen Carol?" I asked. Everybody said no.

I noticed a girl coming out of the ladies room and I stopped her and asked if there was anybody else in there.

"I wasn't really paying attention," she said.

"Well, you mind sticking your head back in there and checking? We're waiting on somebody."

"No problem," she said.

She disappeared into the restroom again and came back out ten seconds later shaking her head. "It's empty," she said.

I thanked her and decided to go look outside.

Out in the parking lot, I looked around. There were a few people walking out to a car, joking and laughing as they went. I didn't see Carol until I peered across the dark parking lot to where our car was. She was standing by the door with her head down and her hand on the handle. When I saw her it brought back that chill I'd felt earlier in my room, the one I'd been trying to ignore ever since. She'd ridden up in the backseat on the passenger side, but she was standing at the backseat driver's side door. I had the very clear sense that it was the wrong spot to be riding in on the way home. I also knew that she knew that. I didn't have the guts to say anything to her. I knew what that would have meant for me.

She was on a mission. She was going to fulfill that mission and, in the process, do something inexplicable and remarkably courageous. This would be something I would be profoundly and forever grateful for but something I wouldn't truly understand for decades to come.

Carol and I were in the backseat, and Bob had Zeppelin's *Physical Graffiti* in the tape player. We only had about fifteen miles to go to get to my place when a car pulled up next to us on our right, the driver gunning his engine over and over. I remember the car vividly. It was a beige 1974 Dodge Dart with a black hardtop. Bob slowed down a bit, hoping he would keep moving on. Then the Dodge slowed down. We sped up, and so did the Dodge. Then Bob slowed down again. The Dodge slowed down next to us, all the while aggressively taunting us to race him.

"Really, race?" said Bob. "We're in a station wagon. Come on!" He turned to me. "What do I do?"

I smirked and shook my head. "Speed up a little again. Maybe we can lose him."

But when Bob put on some speed, so did the Dodge. We couldn't lose him. I was getting nervous, and I could tell everybody else was too. We couldn't really see who was in the car, but there were two people.

Then as Bob slowed down again, the Dodge swerved suddenly, barely crossing over into our lane. Fortunately, Bob saw it coming. He served quickly and was able to avoid a collision.

"What the hell is this guy doing?" said Bob. "We didn't do anything to him."

"Just keep driving," I said. "We're almost to my place. Just watch the asshole."

"Maybe we should pull over," said Carol. "Or just turn around and go the other way." There was real worry in her voice.

"Don't worry, Carol. Everything's going to be fine. Just lay down and put your head in my lap." Then for some reason I said, "It will all be over in a few minutes."

What the hell did I even mean by that? I didn't even know why I'd said it.

Bob sped up again to try and lose the Dodge. And the Dodge sped up again. The driver again swerved intentionally in our lane. Bob saw it coming, but the Dodge had swerved so far that he had no place to go except off the road onto the grassy median. We ended up in oncoming traffic and got hit broadside by an oncoming car. Then everything went dark and stayed that way for a long time.

CHAPTER **21**

WHIRLPOOL TO BLACKNESS

Your mind protects you in strange ways. I think I blacked out because the pain was too intense. I recall being awake for a brief moment, looking up at the night sky, clear and starry, but obscured by the cloudiness in my mind. All other activity and noise faded away. I think I was drifting in and out of consciousness for a moment.

And then I heard a man's voice. "Where do you hurt?" Behind him I could hear emergency radio chatter and the idling engines of the big emergency vehicles.

I felt a pain in my lower back beyond anything I'd felt or imagined. I couldn't really get anything or anyone in focus. It was just a blur.

"Where does it hurt?" said the man.

"My back," I cried out. "My lower back."

I vaguely remember being moved onto a hard board. I passed out again. "When I came to the next time, I heard a different man's voice. He seemed to be speaking slowly, like his battery was running down. "Rooobeeeert," he said. "Can you heeeeeeaaaar me?" Behind this man, the sounds were different—the beeping of medical equipment.

I struggled to open my eyes, and I saw the silhouette of a man against bright lights. As my eyes adjusted and focused, I saw that he was dressed in scrubs and was pulling on a pair of surgical gloves. He spoke like a business man. "Robert, you were in a bad car accident. Your left femur is broken. You have two choices. One, you can be in traction for six months. Two, we can operate and put rods in your leg. Which is it going to be?"

Even in my current state, the answer seemed obvious. I opened my mouth to speak, but my tongue felt dry, and I had a hard time forming the one-word answer. Finally, I managed to whisper, "Rods."

Almost immediately, someone slipped a plastic cup over my nose and mouth. I felt a warm euphoria rush through me. And then nothing.

When I woke up, I had no idea how long I'd been out. My guess would have been a couple of days. I had a hard time focusing on anything other than the fact that I was very sore all over. Maybe it was the drugs I was on, but none of what was going on seemed real to me. I wondered if I'd just dreamed it all.

I couldn't figure out how to even think about it. I could hear footsteps echoing in the hallway outside the room. A woman in a nurse's uniform was sitting at a desk fifteen feet away talking on the phone. Somewhere in the distance a gameshow was playing on TV.

Another nurse appeared at my bedside and began writing something on a clipboard. I managed to ask her to tell me where the hell I was.

"ICU," she said without looking away from what she was writing.

"Huh?"

Then she looked at me. "Intensive care unit, sweetie. Don't worry. We're gonna take good care of you."

"So this is real?" I thought I'd asked it out loud, but she didn't respond, so maybe I didn't. She just wandered off.

The pain in my back had dissipated, but my leg was throbbing. It was hurting in several places. That seemed real. I later figured out that the two spots that hurt the worst were the places where they'd cut me open.

After a while another nurse wandered by, and I managed to get her attention. "What happened?" I said.

"You were in a bad car accident. You're in Good Shepherd Hospital, in Barrington."

"Where are my friends?"

She didn't seem happy with the question. "I don't know, hun. Somebody will be by to talk to you."

I was actually relieved. If she didn't know where my friends where, that must have meant they weren't in the hospital. I was thankful they hadn't been seriously hurt.

After she left, I managed to get hold of the bedside phone. I wanted to call Carol's home. I figured maybe she could explain what had happened. I punched up Carol's number and waited while it rang, eager to hear her voice and to let her know I was okay. Her sister answered, which was odd, since she was rarely home.

"Hi, Kelly, this is Robert," I said. "Can I talk to Carol?"

"You bastard!" she screamed.

Her voice was so loud that I had to hold the phone away from me to keep her from blowing out my eardrum. Still I could clearly hear what she was saying. "You killed my sister. You murderer!" Then I could hear her sobbing.

I couldn't understand what she was talking about. Carol had to have gone home after the accident. That was why she wasn't at the hospital. My mind was racing a mile a minute. But why was her sister so confused. How could she have made such a terrible mistake? The cops or somebody had gotten their wires terribly crossed and given out some bad information. What a terrible blunder. I could feel adrenaline rushing through my veins. I could feel sweat break out on my forehead, and I started breathing heavily. I wanted Kelly to calm down and listen to me so I could tell her Carol was okay. But Kelly continued to scream at me for a few more seconds, and then she just hung up.

I called my mom. I counted the rings. An eternity seemed to pass between each, but on only the third, Mom answered.

"Mom," I said in a panic. "Kelly, Carol's sister. She said Carol was dead. I know that can't be. Can you tell me what the hell is going on? Where is Carol?"

My mom said, "I'm on my way to the hospital now. I'll be there in a few minutes."

What did that mean? Why couldn't she just explain it to me over the phone? The worst feelings I had ever felt in my life were starting to settle upon me like a dark night. Soon I gave up trying to deny what had happened. I was overtaken by grief and disbelief. How could this be? Why did this happen?

I spent thirty minutes alone in hell, and then my mom arrived. She walked into the room crying. The closer she got to me, the more she cried, until she was almost hysterical. She reached me at bedside and said, "Robert, honey, Carol died in the accident."

Carol's sister had been right. She was dead. I couldn't keep it together any longer, and I started sobbing uncontrollably too. I couldn't stop. I couldn't believe it.

But my mom wasn't finished delivering the news. "Robert, Bob died too."

And then I stopped crying. I think for a few minutes I was just in shock. Carol had meant everything to me. She was the dearest love I'd ever had. But Bob wasn't just one of the few decent friends I'd had in life; he was my best friend. Living without either of these people in my life seemed inconceivable, but to have lost both of them in the same night ....

My heart was pounding, and as the shock passed, I began to cry again. But the tears soon turned to tears of anger.

"Why?" I whispered. I asked it again. And then again. And then I realized I was yelling it. "Those two didn't hurt anyone or do anything wrong. Why did they have to die?"

We'd thought we were invincible. Things like this didn't happen to people like us. We were just kids.

The nurse on the ward got up from the desk and returned to my bedside, realizing I'd taken in the news she'd declined to tell me. Before I realize what was happening she'd injected something into my IV, and immediately, against my will, I calmed down.

Selfishly I thought my world was turned upside down again. In the aftermath, I didn't reach out to the others affected the way I should have. I'd never met Bob's parents prior to the accident, but I later had tremendous regret for not visiting them after this accident. I was blinded by my loss and couldn't see past it at the time. I certainly wasn't going to reach out to Carol's family after the phone call with her sister. They hated me. They thought I'd killed their daughter. Killed her? I loved her and was going to marry her.

But in fact, I did feel responsible for her death. I felt like I'd let her die. I'd sensed that something was going to happen. She and I had both known it. Did I do anything about it? Did I say anything to her? Like, let's not go to Wisconsin? No. Did I open a discussion with her about what I knew we both felt that night and why we were feeling it? No. I wish I could ask her now so that I'd know why she sacrificed herself for me. Why?

When I came out of the bar the night of the accident, I saw her waiting to get into the driver's side of the backseat. That was the seat I'd ridden up in, and that's where I would have sat if she hadn't gotten in there. At the moment I saw her, I knew what it meant. She knew she was taking my place. I don't know why. Maybe she'd entered into a soul contract before she was born in which she agreed to sacrifice herself for me when the moment came. This happened long before I ever heard of soul contracts, but I always believed this to be true without knowing what to call it. To this day, I feel in my heart she took her action so I'd have the chance to do something in my life that would benefit many people. I know it had to have happened for a reason. There was too much of a sense of knowing of what was going to happen on both our parts. It's an anomaly, but this sort of thing does happen.

As I lay in the hospital bed that day, I had no spiritual understanding. I only knew that my whole world had gone black. I certainly didn't understand death. But one thing I came to realize that day—I wasn't invincible. Nobody is.

They say you never know when you're going to die. Not true. Some of us do. Carol did. I knew from my inner voice what was going to happen, but I tried to deny it. Since then, I often asked myself who this inner voice is that always talks to me (talks to all of us). Maybe it's our higher self, God within, our subconscious mind trying to guide us, but so frequently we don't listen. I've come to realize that listening to our higher self guides us away from suffering, from potential pitfalls, but when we don't listen, the suffering doesn't end. It continues.

Maybe I should have asked Carol what she was feeling about going to Wisconsin. Now I realize how important it is to recognize feelings, trust your heart, and operate from that trust. I believe we'd all be so much happier if we trusted our instincts and believed in what our hearts are telling us. Our hearts only speak the truth.

Sometimes the solution to a scary situation is so easy. Just pull over and stop. Would that have been so hard that night? It's easy to solve the problem in retrospect. I wish I'd seen it then. Things would have turned out so differently. But it was meant to be this way.

CHAPTER **22**

SURVIVOR'S GUILT

Guilt is a heavy emotion that often leads to severe depression. I had the worst guilt in world. I felt I was responsible for the death of Carol because I dragged her along on the trip to Wisconsin. And I felt responsible for Bob's death, too, because he asked me what to do on the road that night, and I didn't give him the right advice. I remained hospitalized for two weeks. I couldn't do anything except lay there in bed and dwell on what I'd done. Whatever I'd suffered as physical trauma in that car wreck was nothing compared to the emotional beating I suffered in that bed, minute by minute. The nurses flitted in and out, gave me my meds, and checked my vitals. They tried to engage me in some conversation, but I just didn't have it in me. My doctor checked in on me frequently. He tried to counsel me, to encourage me to move past the tragedy.

I had no idea what he was talking about. Move past it? It was in my heart. Was I supposed to cut my heart out? It was extremely difficult for me to understand why had it happened and, maybe more importantly, why was I still alive when I was the one who was responsible? I felt certain I should be dead and Carol and Bob should have been alive.

I was sure my life was less worth saving than theirs. I would have given my life for them in a heartbeat. But, in fact, I was convinced Carol had consciously given her life for me. I wanted to think my life had purpose or that I had some special mission to fulfill. I didn't want to think Carol sacrificed her life for mine if my life wasn't going to amount to much, or to anything, for that matter. I didn't want her to have died in vain. My life had been a tremendous struggle until I'd met Carol. She was a light to me. If she'd died so that my life could continue, I wanted my life to mean something. I wanted to help people.

But how was a person like me going to help anyone? What kind of purpose could my life have? I dropped out of high school. Later, after getting my GED, I'd washed out of college. I had no one in my life who truly cared about me. I was barely eking out an existence as a human being, I should have been dead nearly half a dozen times already. How was I going to get past the trauma of losing Carol, let alone be of use to anyone else?

My mood was dark and my outlook not much better. The nurses in the hospital seemed extra nurturing, caring, and kind to me. But while their lives continued, mine seemed to have shut down. Besides my broken femur I also had some internal injuries. My recovery was slow, perhaps because of my emotional state and hopeless attitude.

A couple of days into my hospital stay, Carol's funeral took place. I wanted to attend. I knew her family was extremely upset at me, and I didn't want to cause them any more grief. I still wanted to go, I just didn't want to face her family.

So with that in mind, I got permission from my doctor to leave the hospital for a few hours as long as I stayed in a wheelchair. My mom called the funeral home to make arrangements for me to come before the wake. I went in the morning before anyone else got there.

As I was helped out of the van and into the wheelchair, I kept hoping that this was a sick practical joke someone was playing on me. I fanaticized that I'd go into the funeral home and Carol would be standing there with a big smile on her face. I still couldn't believe she was dead.

We entered the funeral home, and I was wheeled into the entrance of the parlor where the open coffin stood. Soft music was playing, and there were lots of flowers near the coffin. It struck me that all this had been arranged to make people more at ease with the fact that a loved one had died. It seemed useless.

From my angle, all I could see was the strawberry-blonde hair rising above the edge of the coffin. As I was pushed closer and closer, I was able to see her body and her face. Finally, I was right next to the coffin and looking directly at her face. My mom left me in the room alone with her. I whispered her name. I truly believed she was going to sit up any minute, so I waited. She didn't move. I kept waiting. She wore a lovely blue dress, and her hair and makeup were done just right, as if she'd done the work herself. I had to remind myself that wasn't possible. I tenderly touched Carol's arm. I moved my hand up her arm to her shoulder. Then I caressed her cheek. I leaned over and gently kissed her. Her body was still and cold. The once vibrant young woman I knew and deeply loved lay there lifeless.

She was the one I was planning on spending the rest of my life with, and now she was just an empty shell. It was surreal to me. I was praying, waiting for her to open her eyes so everything would be okay between us, and then this horrific nightmare would be over. Tears streamed down my face as I woke to the grim reality that Carol was not going to open her eyes ever again, or hold my hand, embrace me, or tell me she loved me.

I saw it as life's cruelty. It was cruel to me but also to Carol and her family and everyone who cared for her. I was so inexperienced in life. I did not have the tools to even put it in perspective. For all the horrible tragedies I'd been through, I realized this was the only real crisis I'd ever had to face. Life's road had turned sharply, and I couldn't see past the hill directly in front of me. I knew I'd have to climb that hill, but I didn't know how to do it or what I'd see when I got to the top. But I was to find out that the day of Carol's funeral was to become a force in my life that would drive me to find my purpose.

CHAPTER 23

ONE BRAVE
DECISION

After I got back to the hospital the day of Carol's funeral, a few of my friends from Republic Lumber who'd heard about the accident wanted to come by to visit me. I was so caught up in what was happening in my own head that I couldn't appreciate these people, who took time out of their schedules to visit me because they thought of me as their friend. Instead, I went off on them.

"I do not want to see anyone," I yelled. "Leave me alone!"

This is something I'd regret the rest of my life. I really misunderstood friendship and the meaning of a friend.

Finally, the day came for me to leave the hospital for good. But as the nurses were trying to put me in a wheelchair to take me downstairs, I experienced a tremendous pain in my leg. It was so bad that it was keeping me from getting into the wheelchair. They settled me back into the bed.

"What do you think is happening, Robert?" said one of them.

"What do I think is happening? I think my leg is messed up."

"More messed up than it was yesterday?"

I figured out what she was saying. Maybe the pain, a large portion of it, was psychological. Maybe the thought of going home, back to all those memories, may have had something to do with it. The pain sure felt real enough to me. At any rate, the doctor came to check on me, and after talking it over with me and the nurses, he changed his mind about sending me home. He told me I'd be staying for another night. But the next day, bound and determined, I managed to get into the wheelchair and get out of the hospital.

At home, I spent a week just laying around, watching TV, listening to the stereo. Occasionally a song would come on that reminded me of Carol, and I'd have to change the station before the weight of it crushed me. A week after I got home, I was summoned to the coroner's inquest for the accident. The parents of John, the other kid in the car, drove him and me there.

The meeting took place in a small, dingy room with a conference table and a few cheap chairs. Two guys in suits and one lady sat on one side of the table, and John and I sat on the other side. One guy opened a file folder and started reading a report. At first it was just factual information—make of the car, name of the owner, etc. Then he read a line that blew me away. It said essentially that the primary purpose of the inquest was to figure out which insurance company was going to pay. I was enraged, but I held my tongue. Then he read something that was a quote from the report of the first cop on the scene. He'd written that we'd been drag racing with the other car, which left the scene of the accident.

That was more than I could take. "Bullshit!" I said. "You're crazy!" I managed to stand on my weakened legs, keeping my hands on the table to brace myself. "My girlfriend and my best friend are dead, and you're worried about which insurance company is responsible. And drag racing? We weren't fucking drag racing, you fucking bastards!" I hobbled out of the room on my crutches.

A few days later, an article about the inquest appeared in the paper. "In their testimony, the two men who'd been passengers in Henderson's car denied he was drag racing. In the end, the coroner's jury ruled that

Henderson was not drag racing. The jury also discussed the possibility of filing reckless homicide charges against the driver of the Dart and recommended the police continue their investigation, including their search for the car and its driver."

I was thrilled that they got the story straight.

Over the course of my recovery, I was on crutches for six months. I fought with severe depression, reclusiveness, and suicidal tendencies. I was constantly wondering why I was still alive while Carol and Bob were gone. Since I had nothing but time during my recovery, I kept thinking over and over again about the accident and everything that happened that day. It started to make sense in its own perverted way. Carol and I looking at each other in my room and knowing something was going to happen. Me riding on the driver's side on the way up and her waiting at the car door with her head down on the driver's side when we got out of the bar. It all was coming together like a puzzle. But I could not see the big picture just yet.

I was one man. She wasn't doing this to save a hundred men, ten, or even two men. Just one. Me. A soul for a soul. That didn't add up in my book, especially when what she did was so premeditated. The question remained: Why did she save my life?

The question lingered for many years, but today I believe I'm at a point where I can at least try to answer it. Maybe it just happened, and there was no intent to save my life. That was one thought someone came up with. I considered it briefly, and then I rejected it. It's not what I believe to be true. I believe there was a purpose to what happened, mostly because it's been a driving force for me. I'm committed to making sure Carol didn't die in vain. I've sometimes entertained the notion that it should have happened decades earlier (but I'm a slow learner). But in reality, everything happens when it's supposed to happen, like you reading this book for instance.

The bottom line is that all the experiences I went through in my life have made me passionate about helping others. I believe I'm supposed to use my experiences to help others. That allows me to believe that what Carol did had a meaning, had a purpose.

As I began writing this book, after more than thirty years of thinking about it, I finally decided to do something I'd been avoiding all that time. I decided to go and meet Bob's parents. I had to do a little research to find out if they were still living in Arlington Heights after all these years. Once I did, and through public records research at the library, I located their address. I left the library, hopped in my car, and headed over to their house. It was only about five minutes from Republic Lumber, where Bob and I had worked. I found the place, but I drove by once to assess the situation. Then I turned around and passed it by again. I pulled over to the side of the road. I'd been so consumed with just finding them that I hadn't even considered what I'd say. So I had to think about that. My heart was pounding, and my breathing got very shallow. I was nearly hyperventilating. After all these years, I wasn't sure how they'd respond to me. I didn't want to upset anyone; I just wanted to do something I should have done more than thirty years ago.

I pulled away from the curb where I'd stopped and eased up into their driveway. I noticed they had some children's toys in the yard, which made me think of a young couple. I was hoping I was at the right house.

I went up to the front door. As I reached out to knock, through the screen door I saw an elderly couple sitting in a couple of recliners.

"Who is it?" the woman said before I could knock.

"I'm Robert. I was wondering if I could talk to you for a few minutes."

"What's it about?"

I took a deep breath. This was something I had to do. "I was one of the kids that was involved in the car accident with your son, Bob."

The woman struggled up out of her chair, lifting the years she carried on her back. The man remained motionless in his chair. She crossed to the door slowly and opened it. "Come on in," she said. They both greeted me, and she asked me to have a seat on the couch.

Bob's dad was a big man. Probably about six-foot five and 270 pounds. Behind a full gray beard and mustache, the face seemed to be Bob's. It was definitely his father. I noticed a long scar on his right leg that ran alongside his knee. A cane leaned up against the table. Something about the way he held himself made me think he was more than just old and injured. Like his wife, he was weighed down by the past.

I glanced around the room. All the furniture was at least thirty years old. It was like they'd stopped living when Bob died. I saw the pictures of loved ones on the wallpapered walls and side tables. Prominently displayed were several pictures of Bob. Some were of him as a kid. Others seemed to have been taken within a year of his death. Suddenly I was back in the seventies. All of us, Bob's parents, Bob, and I, were frozen in time.

I started right in. "My intention in coming here today was to not cause you any more grief or open any old wounds."

Bob's mother gave me a sad smile. "The wounds never healed."

I swallowed hard. "I'm sorry, ma'am. After the accident, I was so caught up in my own self-pity, I never stopped to think how everyone else was feeling. Bob was the best friend I had, and I always wanted to come and apologize to you and tell you what a great guy your son was. I also wanted to let you know that we were not drag racing that night. I know there were rumors at the time, but they weren't true. Another car was being reckless and taunting us. Your son did everything he could do to avoid being hit by the other car. They eventually forced us across the median into oncoming traffic. Bob did everything he could to control the car, but it was impossible. He was a great kid."

"I know he was. He was my baby," she said as she started weeping. "He built that screen porch you came up on the week before he died. He said to me, 'I just wanted to get it done this week.' He was determined to get it done as quickly as possible." She told me there wasn't a day that went by that she didn't think of him.

His dad would only would chime in now and then, concurring with his wife or avowing that things just sometimes worked out the way they did.

We talked for about thirty minutes. They both were very gracious and thanked me very much for coming. Bob's dad couldn't get up because of his leg, but his mom did. Mr. Henderson put out his hand, and I grabbed it and held his arm with my other hand.

"Thanks very much for allowing me to talk with you," I said. "I'm sorry I didn't come before. I held out my hand for Bob's mom to shake, but she pulled me in and gave me a hug. We wept in each other's arms.

CHAPTER **24**

AWARENESS OF
DESTINY

I n the immediate aftermath of the accident, I just couldn't shake that I felt I was responsible and didn't deserve to live. I know now that they call it survivor's guilt. About four months after I left the hospital, I reached my breaking point. I didn't want to continue to live. I didn't feel like I deserved to live. My life up until that point had been nothing but trouble. And now I was all broken up, physically and emotionally. I couldn't really do anything. I just moved, painfully, from the living room to my bedroom. Back and forth every few hours. I'd lay on my bed and listen to music, which all seemed to suck. And then I'd lay on the couch and watch TV, which was even worse. All these stupid people in the shows I watched went on living their shallow lives, not realizing how ridiculous their lives were. It was all fiction, but it seemed like the way people I knew really lived. It was meaningless.

One afternoon, as some idiot on TV droned on about solving some fictional crime in some fictionally heroic way, my eyes went from the TV to the coffee table. And on the table stood my bottle of painkillers. I'd just gotten the prescription refilled. I knew how many pills were in the bottle. Enough. I sat up and snatched the bottle off the table, struggled to my feet, and began hobbling out of the room on my crutches.

When I got into my room, I swung the door shut behind me, but it didn't close. I looked over my shoulder, and there was my mom with her hand on the door.

"Hey," she said. "What are you doing with the meds?"

"I need them."

"You just took one twenty minutes ago. You need another one already?"

I scoffed. "No, I don't need another one. I need all of them. I can't take this anymore." I opened the bottle.

Mom rushed toward me and grabbed my wrist. We started wrestling with the bottle, but even with my injuries, I was stronger than her. I finally broke free.

She took a couple of steps back, breathing heavily. "You want to kill yourself, go ahead. I can't take this anymore either. That's all you've been saying. 'I want to kill myself! I want to kill myself!' Go ahead, then." She turned and left the room crying.

I sat down on the bed with the bottle of pills in my hand. Well, this is what you wanted, I thought. Go ahead and get it over with.

I dumped a bunch of pills into my hand and sat there staring at them. I thought about my past, how much crap I'd gone through, why my life had to be so difficult. I felt like I wasn't going to make it past this grieving. Then I started thinking about Carol again, our relationship, our time together, and what she had done to keep me alive. And I came back to the thought that had been haunting me. Carol had knowingly given her life to save mine. If I killed myself, then she would have definitely given her life in vain.

Then out of nowhere I thought of 1984. I wondered what this meant and why this would come to me at that moment or occasion. I thought if I could just hang on until then, maybe that would be when things would finally change for the better for me. I brought my cupped hand back to the open bottle and listened to the pills rattle back into it.

I've since come to understand that the judgment we render for ourselves is the worst kind of judgment there is, and it sometimes leads us to do terrible things. It leads us to feel like we're at the end of our rope. When you're in that position and someone tells you to hang in there, it sounds ridiculous. But here's a universal law I've learned. If you're at the end of your rope and you keep hanging in there, more rope will always appear. It's a universal law that you will never have to deal with more than you can handle. Although it certainly didn't seem that way at the time, I could and did handle it.

I had a lot of anger about my life in general. I also just refused to play by the rules society played by. My friends thought I was crazy when I would tell them about things I'd do. Like chasing cops who were speeding. I did that more than a few times, but one night in particular stands out in my mind.

I was driving down the highway minding my own business when a cop car came past me doing something like eighty in a fifty-five-mile-an-hour zone. No lights, no siren, just a whole lot of accelerator.

My belief had always been that cops should obey the law they're trying to enforce. So I was determined to enforce the law on this guy. I stepped on the gas and slowly but surely ate up the distance between us. When I settled in behind him, I started flashing my headlights and honking my horn. It was the best I could do without roof lights and a siren.

The cop slowed down, at first probably just to see who the nut job was who was chasing him down. He let me pull even with him, and then I started waving for him to pull over. Finally he tapped his brakes so that I had to pass him. He pulled in behind me and hit his roof lights and siren and pulled me over.

When he approached my car, I rolled down my window.

"Do you know how fast you were going?" he said, shining a flashlight in my face.

"Do you know how fast *you* were going, Officer?" I said. "'Cause I had to punch it to catch up with you."

Well, I guess that made him angry. "You don't need to be catching up with me, buddy."

I started counting off his violations on the fingers of my hand sticking out through the window. "You had no siren. You had no roof lights. You were doing at least eighty at one point. And you obviously weren't going anywhere important, 'cause you've got time to stop and talk to me."

He laughed, but it wasn't because he thought I was funny. "Well, I got someplace important to be now." And he pointed to the ground he was standing on. "Let me see your license and registration, hot shot." Of course he gave me a ticket.

The next day I called the department he worked for and asked about any emergencies that had happened in that area at the time he ticketed me. There were none. I wrote up my notes on the call, and when my court date arrived, I explained the whole thing to the judge. He threw the ticket out. I couldn't help but flash the cop a smile on my way out of the courtroom.

CHAPTER 25

CONTACT FROM BEYOND

The insurance company settled for the accident, and I received about $12,000. Money should give you a new start in theory. It can be life changing, and I intended to use the money in a wise way and make a new start for myself. I thought of taking my mom's suggestion, which was to take some much needed time to get away, take a train out west to Colorado, and see the country. Or maybe I'd buy a car or invest in a condo. But I was young, dumb, and had greasy fingers. I was not responsible with money, and this paradigm inside me wasn't allowing me to get out of my comfort zone. At the time, it didn't want me to take chances in life. I didn't go on any trips or use it to develop myself.

The few "friends" I had knew I received a settlement from the accident, and they started hanging around me more. Partly at their urging, the money was being used on drugs. For a while, I got caught up in it. I was really partying. But after about six months of that life, I was broke once again. Soon my so-called friends disappeared. I realized that these people were never really my friends. They were the people I tried to replace Bob with.

But they were nothing like Bob, who was a good, sincere friend. In fact, they were nothing like any of the good friends I once knew at Republic Lumber. They were only concerned about themselves and having a good time.

With the money gone, and now another cold December setting in, I decided I was going to start getting my body into shape. I bought some weights and started working out. Since I didn't have a job at the time, I was able to work out six days a week for two to three hours a day. I only took Sundays off. I stopped drinking too. For six months, my only focus was getting in shape. My body was starting to feeling stronger and look a lot better than it ever had before. Up to then, this was the only thing I'd actually stuck with consistently.

Since I played some high school football—and I missed the opportunity to play in Hawaii—I thought if I got into shape I could go try out for the team at Harper College, the local community college. I had soft hands as a receiver and could catch just about anything that was thrown my way. While working out, I thought about football and watched it on TV to help motivate me. This became my primary reason to get into shape.

There wasn't a day that went by that I didn't think about Carol. I was reeling from her loss and continued to feel very attached to her. I missed her. I still wondered what I was supposed to be doing with my life. I wondered if I was doing the right thing. What would my life be like if she was still here with me? Since I needed to work and didn't own a car, I found a job at a gas station within walking distance. It wasn't much of job, but at least it was something.

February rolled in and with it the typical brutal Illinois winter weather. At work one dark, snowy night with ten inches of snow already on the ground and the snow still coming down sideways, I was settling in for an easy night. Nobody in their right mind would be out in this weather. I was going to be collecting a paycheck for just sitting on my ass. I could see through the big picture window that nothing was happening outside. Not a car in sight. Suddenly the door whipped open. Then, as the cold wind howled inside the station and the snow blew in with it, a beautiful woman strolled in. When that woman walked into the station, I felt as if I'd entered some sort of parallel dimension of time and space. I was spooked. I had gooseflesh. I couldn't believe my eyes. The resemblance to Carol was uncanny. I gasped. She looked real, but she couldn't be real. Was this a ghost? Perhaps she'd transcended or materialized from another dimension. Considering the connection we'd had and the way mystical energy surrounded her death, part of me really believed I was receiving a visit from beyond. She had the same build as Carol, same nice round cheeks, same complexion, same length and color of hair. I had never seen another girl with the exact same hair color or permanent wave in her hair like Carol. She even sounded like her.

I told myself there was no such thing as ghosts, but if that were true, maybe this was actually Carol. Could she have been alive? Was it all some weird mistake? If this was Carol, who was that at the funeral home? I was wishing—no, diligently praying—that this was real and she'd come back to tell me everything was just a crazy dream and that she was there to wake me up and bring me back to reality. My mind was racing, searching for answers and trying to make sense out of this surreal state I was in. I thought of asking her what her name was, but I was so afraid she would say "Carol." If she did, I wouldn't know how to deal with it. I probably would have passed out.

I decided to ask anyway. "What's your name?"

She blew on her cold hands for a moment, leaving me in an agony of anticipation waiting for her answer. Finally she said, "Eve." Her voice had a relaxing, soothing tone.

I was relieved she didn't say Carol, but I was a little disappointed too. Regardless of her name, I truly felt I was in Carol's presence.

I looked out the big window again and still didn't see a car. "Where's your car, Eve?"

"I walked here. I just got off work." She hitched her thumb in the direction she'd come from.

Why would anyone be walking in these blizzard conditions? I was intrigued by this woman. She unzipped her coat, and then I saw it. She was in her work uniform. It was the same yellow, gold, and green checked waitress dress Carol used to wear. She worked at the same place Carol had, just four blocks away. Oddly, she didn't look that cold and didn't have any snow covering her. And she had no hat, no gloves, and no boots. She actually looked like she was warm.

"What brought you in here?" I asked, half expecting her to tell me she had a message from … from what? The universe? God?

"My mom was going to pick me up here," she said in a comforting voice. "Eve, you look like someone I once knew."

She didn't seem surprised, but she gave me a look that seemed to suggest I'd said the right thing. "Oh, really?" she said.

I was profoundly moved and had to struggle to hold back my emotions. Her presence brought back a lot of feelings and deep emotions for Carol that I'd suppressed, like everything else in my life, which I never properly dealt with.

I wanted to know more about Eve. Part of me still wondered if she really was Carol. There were too many strange, unexplainable things in the way she'd popped in like she had, especially on a night like that.

I was about to ask if she'd known Carol from work, but before I could, she tilted her head toward the door. "My mom's here," she said.

I looked out through the window. No cars had pulled up. "Where?"

"Over there," she said, and she pointed to the stores next to the station.

Why would she park over there? It was forty yards away. She'd have to walk through the nearly knee-deep snow.

I didn't want her to leave the station. I wanted her to stay until the questions I had were all answered and I found out more about this mysterious woman. As I watched her walk out of the station and get into her mom's car, with a light snow still drifting down through the streetlights, it was if Eve and her mom just disappeared, faded to white in the snowy night. In some strange way, I felt as if I'd lost Carol again, yet I had an unexplainable feeling of comfort as well. During this entire experience, not one customer, or one car for that matter, was anywhere near the station.

When I thought about this night later, I came to believe Carol was trying to tell me not to worry about her, that she was fine and that I needed to move on with my life. It was hard to think of letting go, but after this experience I was able to loosen my grip on Carol's memory, and I was able to take a few steps forward with my life.

CHAPTER **26**

WHO SAVED
WHOM

T he moving job would change my life in ways I could never imagine.
I needed a different job. Work at the gas station was boring as hell,
and it didn't pay much either, and since my leg had healed for the most part
and I was stronger from working out, I decided to ask my brother-in-law to
get me a job at his moving company. He made lots of money and occasional
traveled across the country, and I thought this would be something I'd like.

"Sorry, Rob," he said over beers one night. "They only hire people
with experience."

I didn't get what he was talking about. This was just labor, not rocket
science. "Well, how do I get that experience?" I said.

"Go to work for U-Haul. They just started hiring labor."

I looked into it to see what they paid, and it wasn't nearly what my
brother-in-law's job was paying. And he was talking about quite a cruise.
It was thirty miles from my home to U-Haul. Still, it made sense. If I
wanted a good job with good money, I had to pay my dues. So ... I got a
job at U-Haul.

I started out doing all the grunt work—moving the heaviest stuff, carrying furniture and heavy boxes to third- and fourth-floor apartments in Chicago, never getting to drive. Yeah, I was paying my dues all right. Everyone hired us. We were cheap labor. People were smart to use us—bust someone else's back instead of their own. Sometimes it wasn't so bad. Occasionally we spent a day or two driving around a couple of states, bringing more trucks back to our store. Those were easy, restful, and much-appreciated days.

When I'd been there for three months, I figured I had enough experience to get that job with my brother-in-law. It seemed like it was all the same thing—labor. So how much experience did I really need? But I was glad I'd stuck with it for as long as I did because one of the last jobs I did at U-Haul changed the way I looked at everything.

For a couple of years before taking that job, even though I would try and ignore them, I'd been having strange, fleeting thoughts. I'd get a feeling like I was in a life-threatening situation, or I'd sense that I was about to have to give CPR to someone or do something to save their life. I always just shook the feeling off and went on with whatever I was doing. I hoped I wouldn't be put in that kind of situation. I didn't want to be responsible for saving anyone when I couldn't even take care of myself.

One midsummer day I went into work like any other day. I was the driver that day and partnered with someone I didn't usually work with. After our morning job we were off to Schaumburg. That was great because I would be close to home, and I liked Schaumburg, where I'd spent part of my childhood.

When we arrived, we were relieved to find that the job was on the first floor. We only had a few items, and we could back the truck right up to the patio door and unload. As we got out of the truck, I started having one of those feelings again. I shook my head and told myself it was nothing. As soon as we walked in, we could hear yelling and crying coming from the back bedroom, and it was getting louder. Two women came out of the room. One was yelling hysterically, "My baby! My baby!" She looked at us as if we'd be able to help her.

The other lady came behind her. She was in tears and was carrying the baby girl, which couldn't have been more than three months old.

She was limp and her face was blue. I grabbed my partner's shirtsleeve and pulled him to me. I said in a low voice, "That kid's not breathing. Do something."

He looked at me, alarmed. Then he grabbed the baby and laid her on the Formica counter in the kitchen. He brushed wisps of brown hair back from her forehead as he began to do CPR.

I tried to calm the mother down. "Lady, lady," I said. "Take it easy. Everything will be okay." I didn't really believe this myself. I thought we were too late, because the baby was blue and turning darker. I asked the other woman, "Did you call an ambulance?"

"Yes!" she cried out.

It seemed like five stressful minutes passed, but I realized later it was only about a minute. The baby was not responding. Her entire body had turned as blue as the darkest ocean.

The mother was just bawling. Then she turned to me, her brown eyes glistening with tears. "Please, please! Help my baby! Help my baby!"

Why was she asking me? My partner was already doing CPR, and I had no training in it. But I couldn't deny a mother's plea for help. Still struggling with the darkness and death from my past, I couldn't stand by and let this baby die right in front of me without at least trying.

I approached my partner and said, "Stand aside. Let me try."

I put my hand on the girl's white onesie, which was damp with the sweat from my partner's hand. I tried administering a few breaths, then a few gentle pumps to her fragile chest. Nothing! So I did a few more breaths and a few more gentle pumps. No response.

Still crying and comforting each other, the baby's mother and friend stood with their arms wrapped around one another. They were awakening to the reality that hope for the baby's life was fading like a morning dream.

Don't panic, I thought. I'm not going to let this baby die. I'm not going to let this baby die. I'm not going to let this baby die. I kept saying these words to myself while trying to bring life back to her. I decided to pick her up. I turned her over, cradled her in my left arm, then gave her a few firm thrusts between the shoulder blades. No signs of life.

I tried it again. Still nothing.

"Come on. Come on," I muttered. I gave her three gentle shoves on the back again.

And then I began to hear the baby sucking air into her tiny lungs. I could just barely here it, and then the baby let out the loudest cry of her short little life. It was the most beautiful sound I'd ever heard.

"Oh, my god," I said, and I turned to the mother.

The mother's cries of fear and grief turned instantly to tears of joy and elation. She took the baby from my arms, and I slumped against the wall. I looked up and saw that my partner's mouth was wide open, and he was staring at me. He looked like someone who'd witnessed a miracle. A warm sensation traveled throughout my entire body, as if I was slowly being immersed in a warm tub of water. Then a great peace and calm came over me, as if I were standing in the fields of heaven.

Not more than a minute later, the paramedics arrived.

When they took the baby to check her out, the mother threw her arms around me. She hugged and kissed me and said, "Thank you. Thank you for saving my baby! Thank you!"

The other woman and my partner were explaining to the paramedics what had happened.

One of them turned to me. "Nice job," he said. "You probably saved that baby's life."

I was not proud of myself. Instead, I had a profound sense of humility, gratitude, and joy. That gut feeling I'd been having and that I'd been trying to shake off finally led me to something important. I was thankful that I was in the right place at the right time and that I was allowed to help. This was the first time in my life when I did something that was truly meaningful, that had a purpose. This experience gave me back a small piece of the self-worth I'd lost so many years ago. It also seemed to ignite a sense of purpose within me. Perhaps, on that day, that little baby girl saved my life too.

CHAPTER **27**

JUST ONE
LOOK

I finally felt like I was moving forward when my brother-in-law's company hired me. I knew I could do the work. My looks were deceiving because I was smaller than some of the burly guys there. I was only five ten and 168 pounds, but that was all muscle, and I could hold my own. Some of the other guys were actually surprised at how much I could lift.

The interesting part of this job was that we would work during the day doing residential moves, then, after five o'clock, we could do commercial work in the high-rise offices in the city of Chicago. Even though we sometimes worked twelve- to fifteen-hour days, I was not as tired after work as I'd been after working at U-Haul for eight to ten hours with all the third- and fourth-floor carries. But it still took a toll on my body, some days worse than others. A couple of times, I traveled with some of the long-haul drivers. This was great because I got to see the country. As the helper and not the driver, the money was terrible, but it was a good experience.

One particular haul to the West Coast via the southern states was memorable. It was the beginning of spring, and there was still a chill in the air and patches of snow on the ground along a lot of the route. We stopped in Flagstaff, Arizona, to eat dinner on our second night out. It was a family-type place just off the interstate. A few tables away was a mom and dad and a couple of children. One of the kids was a girl who was maybe twenty, twenty-two. I was fixated on her. She was cute, with blonde hair and glasses. She was happily enjoying her meal and talking to her parents. I couldn't make out what they were saying, but once in a while, one or all of them would laugh out loud. She was still like a kid in some ways, but she was an adult and her parents seemed to accept her as an adult. Her being with her parents at that age made me wonder what my life would have been like if that had been my family.

I wondered what this girl was about, where she lived, if I would ever see her again. When their dishes were cleared, Dad laid a map out on the table. Looked like they were on vacation.

The girl must have felt me staring at her, because she lifted her head and looked toward me. Our eyes meet for the first time, and I sensed I knew this girl. What made me feel like I knew this girl before? Was she a soul mate? I was two thousand miles from home. I didn't know anyone out here. I snapped out of the trance I was in and went on eating with my partner. I never gave it another thought.

My body was paying the price for the hard labor I was doing, but I didn't care. I was making some good money for the first time in my life, and I was finally able to get a place of my own. It was a small, one-bedroom with a glass wall looking out onto the building's atrium. It was just ten minutes from work. When I moved in there, something changed in me. I had my own home, and it looked cool. It was a great place to take the ladies.

And I met a lot of those. My coworkers egged me on, and my ego couldn't always let it go. We'd be on a job site doing a commercial move and there'd be a girl there who worked for the company we were moving.

"Hey, look at her," one of them would say. "Go talk to her. Bet you can't pick her up."

Actually, most of the time I could, but I wanted to believe the search for the right woman was more complicated than that. I was in need of something, lacking something. None of the women I met seemed to be able to supply that, whatever it was. None of them made me happy, like the way I used to feel when I was with Carol. None of them could live up to my expectations.

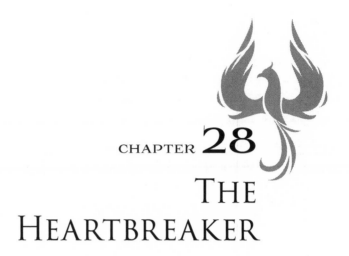

CHAPTER 28

THE
HEARTBREAKER

I was leaving broken hearts all over the state. I didn't mean to break up with all these girls, it just seemed to happen. One girl whose heart I felt especially bad about breaking lived in Schaumburg. The first time I went to her house to pick her up, I met her dad, a construction worker.

"You don't look like a mover," he said sitting in his easy chair in the front room.

I smirked. "What's a mover supposed to look like?"

He folded his newspaper, set it aside, and stood up to make his point. "Bigger than you."

I took offense at that, but I nodded. "You know, you're right. There are guys at work who are bigger than me. But I guarantee you I'm in better shape than they are. I can carry more than most of them."

He rubbed me the wrong way, but I could put up with him for the sake of his daughter. She had long, curly, dark hair and was almost as tall as me and had a great body. I was sincerely attracted to her, but for some reason I couldn't bring that sense of caring, kindness, and thoughtfulness you're supposed to bring to a relationship. I let her get too close to me, then I hurt her deeply, which bothered me a great deal; but I didn't understand how to access the feelings I was supposed to have in those situations.

Generally, I was not concerned about anyone else's feelings except my own. One day she came over to my place because I wouldn't return her calls. She gave me a card telling me how much she cared about me, and she had tears streaming down her check while I read it. Regrettably, I couldn't bring myself to care about or feel any passion for her. I always wished I could meet her again when I got older and apologize for the way I treated her—for not caring and being more considerate of her feelings. What more can I say.

CHAPTER **29**

THE
PROTECTOR

My little sister, Robin, was somewhat of a tomboy, always a little rambunctious. She never hesitated to say what was on her mind. Furthermore, she never used any discernment as to when or where it was appropriate to say what was on her mind. She'd moved out and lived in her first apartment with a roommate. It was a two-story building with a separate outside entrance to each apartment, like an old motel. Her roommate, Sue, had been a friend of hers, but when they lived together they didn't get along, so her girlfriend soon moved to another apartment in the same complex. A few days later, my sister noticed that some of her personal belongings were missing. She insisted that this girl had stolen them, which turned out to be true.

One Friday night, my friend Brad and I were out riding our motorcycles and decided to stop by my sister's to say hello.

She ushered us in and got us each a soda. We sat on her secondhand couch with the fabric wearing thin in places, and she launched into her tale. "Robert, Sue took my stuff, and I know she's over at her apartment now. Let's go over there and get it back from that bitch. She's a thief."

I almost did a spit take. My leather jacket creaked as I leaned forward. "Listen," I said. "I don't want any trouble. I didn't come over to get in any fights or start any problems."

"There won't be any problems. I just want to go over there with you two and ask for my stuff back."

I kept my eyes on my sister, but I held up a hand to Brad in case he started feeling too helpful. "I know you too well. You have a tendency to shoot your mouth off and start trouble."

"I won't. I'm not going to do anything. I just want to ask her for my stuff back, that's all."

I raised my eyebrows. "That's all?"

"That's it."

I didn't have a good feeling about this, and something told me not to go over there. But I didn't listen to myself. I turned to Brad and he shrugged. "Why not?" he said.

So, wearing our leather jackets, we followed my sister out the door and down the stairs of her building.

Before we got to where we were going, I picked up a tube-shaped rock about three inches long and handed it to Brad. My sister was a little ahead of us, and I leaned close to my friend. "I don't have a good feeling about this, so take this rock. Clinch it in your fist and leave it there. Whatever you do, keep it in your fist. Do not let it go."

"Okay," he said.

The other girl's apartment was on the second floor of a two-story building. It was the kind of place with exterior stairs going up from the parking lot to the balcony where all the apartment doors were. As we approached, we could see her standing on the balcony in front of her place with a couple of her male friends. There was a party or something going on inside her apartment. The door behind her was open, and music was playing.

As we were making our way up the stairs, I turned to my sister again. "Remember, Robin, don't shoot your mouth off or start any trouble. Let's handle this calmly."

"Don't worry," she said. "I'm only going to ask her where my stuff is and tell her I want it back."

We got to the top of the stairs and took a couple of steps toward Sue. She saw us and nudged the two guys with her. Robin was on my left, and Brad was on the right.

Before Sue could even say hello, my sister belted out, "Where is the stuff you took from me? I want it back now, you bitch!"

I rolled my eyes but said nothing.

"I didn't take anything from you," Sue yelled back.

"Yes you did, you bitch!"

And then Robin took a swing at the girl. I was thinking, thanks, Robin. As Robin and Sue were wrestling with one another, Sue's friends came at Brad and me and started swinging. We fought back, and I thought we had things pretty much under control, but this was just the beginning. One by one, more of Sue's male friends came out of the apartment onto the balcony. I didn't know how they had all fit inside the apartment. It seemed like an endless stream of guys, and they all wanted to join in the fight. There were ten or eleven of them. This was an all-out assault on us. We handled the first two and knocked them out of the way for a while. Then it was the other eight or nine guys we were concerned about. As I was blocking a punch from one guy, another one punched me right in the mouth. I gave him a left forearm to the face and then punched another guy with my left fist. After that I couldn't keep track. Fists and elbows were flying everywhere. I was getting hit, but I was sure as hell hitting back, too. I caught a glimpse of Robin as she broke away from Sue and came around to stand behind me. Great, I thought. Now she decides to stay out of the way. I gave her a half look over my shoulder. "Just get downstairs," I said. Then I noticed that the stairway was blocked and she really didn't have anywhere to go.

Brad and I were fighting side by side, but we were soon separated. And these other guys didn't fight fair, either. One of them grabbed a beer bottle, broke it on the iron railing of the balcony, and took a swipe at me. I was able to do a "Neo," like in the Matrix. I leaned back and dipped out of the way, but he still managed to scrap the left side of my neck with the jagged edge of the bottle, leaving a three-inch laceration. Blood began oozing out.

That just pissed me off more. I kicked him in the abdomen after his follow through, then gave him a shot in the side of the ribs. Then I punched him once in the face. He fell to the ground. By this time the fight seemed like it was going on for several minutes, but it was probably only one minute or so. I noticed Brad had his hands full, and for the moment so did I. The guy I'd knocked down got back up and joined the other four or more guys that were fighting me. They all jumped on me and had me down. I took a momentary glance at my friend and noticed that five or six other guys had him down on the ground beating him. A couple of them had his arms and were pulling on him. It looked like they were getting ready to launch him over the side of the railing down to the first floor.

Seeing this, I knew I had to get these guys off of me and help Brad. Exerting as much effort as I could, I stood up while fighting the guys off of me. I rushed toward Brad, punching guys along the way. I heard sirens getting closer. Then, with as much strength as I could muster, I leaped into the air and bowled over the top of the five guys who were trying to throw Brad off the balcony. They all took a tumble to the ground.

By the time we hit the ground, the police sirens were loud. I pulled Brad out from among the bodies lying on the ground. "Let's get the hell out of here," I yelled.

My sister led the way down the stairs. Sue's friends started yelling at us, and a couple of them were leaning over the balcony railing to try and hit us while we were going down the stairs. On our way down, I punched one of them on the side of his face for good measure. We got to our motorcycles, hopped on, and rode down to the other end of the complex. Then we tucked the bikes in where they wouldn't be easily seen and hurried into Robin's apartment.

Once we got back up to the apartment, I noticed Brad was hurt.

"It's my shoulder," he said. "It hurts like hell. I can barely move it. I think it's dislocated."

"Other than that, are you okay?" I said.

"Just a little sore." He held out his bloody-knuckled hand. "Here's the rock. I held onto that thing the whole time, like you said."

I chuckled. "Yes, you did. Good job, my man."

Brad glanced at me and then did a double take. "Oh, man. You got a cut on your neck. You better take care of that. It's bleeding."

I touched it and then looked at the blood in my hand. "Yeah, I know. That's where that bastard caught me with that broken beer bottle. It's just a scrape. I'll be fine. Man, those bastards were getting ready to toss you off the balcony."

"Thanks for saving my ass back there."

"Hey, no problem, man. Did you see me dive on those five guys? We did awesome against those guys, man." I realized I was pumped with adrenaline and was probably talking a mile a minute.

After we were done congratulating ourselves for not getting killed, there was the little matter of my sister and her big mouth.

"Robin," I said. "Why did you start yelling at her and take a swing at her? I told you to stay calm and let us handle it, but you couldn't control yourself. You almost got us killed!"

"She lied to me. I'm not taking that from that lying bitch!"

"That's why I didn't want to do this. You always seem to shoot your mouth off and start something. This time I was hoping it would be different."

She shrugged. "You guys are okay, aren't you?"

I looked at her like she was crazy. "Okay? He's got a separated shoulder, we both have bumps and bruises, and I have a scrape on my neck. Sure, Robin. We're okay."

CHAPTER **30**

WORKING OUT
PAYS OFF

One night the following week, Brad and I were back at my sister's again. I'd been working out for six months and was not drinking. Robin had a few girlfriends over too. One kept looking over to check me out, and I was doing the same. Physically, I was in the best shape of my life, but my self-esteem and self-worth were still low.

The TV was on, but the volume was all the way down, and Robin was playing loud music. Everyone was drinking except me. My sister said I should have a beer, and then one of her friends chimed in and said I should. It had been six months since I'd had a drink. I thought about it. Should I? Shouldn't I? Finally, another of Robin's friends, the cutest girl there, urged me to have a beer.

I shrugged. "What the hell? You talked me into it."

"All right," she said with a smile, and she handed me a cold beer.

I took it from her and smiled. "What's your name?"

"Julie," she said.

"Hi, Julie, I'm Rob. I got a bike outside. You want to go for a ride?"

She got a big smile on her face and stood up. I left the beer on the coffee table, and Julie and I headed out. We didn't go far, just tooled around the neighborhood a bit. I opened it up a couple of times and told her to hold onto me tight or she might fall off the back. "I'd hate to have to scrape you off the pavement," I said.

She laughed and held on.

When we got back to Robin's place, she got off the back of the bike and thanked me. "Hey, you want to come over to my place for a pool party tomorrow?" she said.

"Sure, that sounds fun."

"And bring your friend Brad too."

She was a couple of years younger than me and worked as a waitress at the same restaurant where Carol used to work. Julie and I seemed to get along okay. She really didn't have any goals or aspirations in life. She was just taking it day by day.

The next day, Brad and I rode our bikes over to Julie's place. We saw her out by the pool with some of her girlfriends and guy friends.

"You guys can change into your suits in the changing room over there," she said.

"Okay, thanks," I said.

When we got back outside, Julie was sitting by the pool with her legs dangling in the water. Her friends were on the other side of the pool talking to some guys. When we started walking toward her, she saw me for the first time in my suit. I saw her friend look at us and then say something to her. It was a long walk to the pool, so I couldn't hear what she was saying. Julie looked at us and mouthed something across the pool to her girlfriend, like, "Oh, my gosh."

I started feeling a little self-conscious about my appearance. I thought they were making fun out of me for some reason. Soon I realized they were not making fun of me. They were just marveling at my physique.

We sat down by Julie, and her girlfriends came over and introduced themselves to Brad and me. We just hung out and talked and dangled our legs in the cool water. We didn't talk to the other guys much.

Later, when the girls went to the bathroom together, Julie's three guy friends walked over to us. The biggest one came right up to me. He stood towering over me as I sat with my legs still in the water. "I'm not afraid of you," he said in a stern voice.

I was surprised. "What?"

"I'm just telling you, man, I'm not afraid of you."

"Okay, great, pal. Have a nice day." I waited for his friends and him to walk away. Then I turned to Brad. "Wow, she has some nice friends, huh?"

"I think that guy feels intimidated by you."

I pointed to myself. "By me? I didn't do anything for him to feel intimidated by me."

I saw this as fitting into one of the themes of my life. Even if I didn't do anything to ask for it, trouble seemed to follow me, waiting for me in the shadows and then stepping out to surprise me.

"I don't want to fight the guy," I said. "I just came here to relax. Why would he even say that to me, man? It doesn't make any sense."

Brad shook his head and chuckled. "You just showed up, man. Look at yourself. You've been working out for six months. You're not that scrawny little guy anymore. You're in great shape. This guy feels intimidated by you because you're in his territory with all 'his girls.' He's the king here. So that's why he feels threatened by you. He's protecting what he thinks is his."

"Geez, man, I just want to relax. I don't need this bullshit. It's always something. Why does trouble always have to follow me?"

"Relax," said Brad. "He's not going to do anything. Anyway, if he did, you could take him."

We ended up splitting shortly thereafter. Later that day, Julie dropped a bomb on me and told me she had a two-year-old child named Ashley. Julie was eighteen, and in all honesty, she wasn't a good mother. But it had been rough. She'd had the kid when she was sixteen. She was still a child herself and hadn't really had a chance to grow up. Someone had made complaints to the Department of Children and Family Services (DCFS) about Julie and the way she was treating and/or neglecting her child. DCFS had taken Ashley away from her for being an unfit mother and placed her in a foster home. They told Julie the only way she could get her back would be to start being more responsible and provide a stable environment for the child. Although she was upset about it, she was using the time to do what she wanted, which was to have fun and party.

CHAPTER **31**

DETOUR
OF DUTY

I'd always thought the army might give me direction. I think a lot of young men believe the service might be a last resort, but I thought I might find in it the guidance I'd been lacking.

I'd been dating Julie for a few months, and I decided to take a second job for a while to make some extra money. I ended up selling vacuums and met John while I was working there. John couldn't keep still. He always had to be doing something. I just got it in my head that he might benefit from some structure in his life too. I talked to him about my idea of trying to find some direction, and we decided we'd both go into the army. We spoke with a recruiter and found out they had a buddy program that allowed friends to go in and stay together.

We both wanted to go into the Rangers. We talked about how great it would be to travel all over the world while serving our country.

The recruiter scheduled our physical and entrance exams at the MAPS station in Chicago. On that day, John and I took the train in together. The place was big and intimidating. We both made it through the physical part with no hitches. After our examinations, there were some questions about our medical histories. One of the questions was, "Do you have respiratory problems or asthma?" I gave a lot of thought to whether or not to answer it truthfully.

Shortly after the exam, we were sitting in a waiting area, and a recruiter came in and pulled up a chair near us. He was a real squared-away looking guy with a sharp uniform and a buzz cut.

"John," he said, handing him a folder. "You're good to go."

John lit up. "Yeah?" he said.

"There's some paperwork in there you need to read and sign, and we'll get you set up with a date to report, but you're in."

John slapped me on the leg, then he turned to me with a look of concern. He looked at the recruiter. "What about Rob?"

The recruiter took a deep breath. "Yeah, I know you were planning on doing the buddy program, but unfortunately, Rob, we can't take you."

"Why's that?" I said, a bit stunned.

"It's your respiratory history. That disqualifies you." He turned to John and reached out for a handshake. "Congratulations, John."

I felt myself blush. This was another big disappointment for me. Knowing that I needed to get my life back on track, I thought the army was definitely the way to go. They didn't even think I was good enough for them.

John told me how sorry he was that it didn't work out for me, but after he went into the army we lost track of each other. I never heard from him again.

Not being allowed in the army reminds me of an old Chinese parable: "Good news, bad news, how can one say? With our limited understanding, what seems to be bad, it could be good in disguise."

My conscious self had it all figured out with that army thing (at least he thought he did), but I think my higher self was telling me that my destiny lay elsewhere and kept me from dying in some desert in the Middle East.

CHAPTER 32

GAME OF LOVE

They say God works in mysterious ways, and I believe it. Even something as small as a voice on a radio station can be God's favor shining down. Julie and I were driving down the highway coming back from the mall in November, and we heard a commercial for someplace in Florida on the radio.

I looked at her. "Have you ever done anything really spontaneous before?"

"No, not really."

"Have you ever been to Florida?"

She shook her head. "No, I haven't been anywhere."

I took my right hand off the wheel and put it on her knee. "Do you want to go?"

She stared at me for a moment. "When?"

"Right now!"

She squinted at me. "Are you serious?"

"Of course. Do you want to go?"

"Yes!"

I smacked the steering wheel with my hand. "Okay, we're going!"

I had quit selling vacuums. I still had the moving job, but I had a long weekend off ahead.

We went home, and I called the airline and got a couple of tickets. We left that evening. We made a long weekend out of it and visited Disney World. Since Ashley was still with her foster family she wasn't able to go with us. It was a great vacation, and we really needed it.

Back at home, during the time we spent with little Ashley, I figured out that I was a much better parent to her than Julie was. I could relate to that little girl, despite the circumstances she was born into. I wanted to help her grow up in a good environment.

DCFS wanted a stable home life for little Ashley. After a couple of months, Julie and I talked and decided we'd move in together to help establish stability in the home for Ashley. This would make it easier for me to encourage Julie to be more responsible. That sounds like an oxymoron, but at the same time I figured it would facilitate getting Ashley home faster. This was a time in my life when being a father was the furthest thing from my mind. All I wanted was to get Ashley back; I really didn't want to be a father. As the months went on, Julie and I would drive to the city for supervised visits with Ashley and DCFS counselors. We were working together as a "couple," doing what we had to do to get her back. After nearly a year, Julie was able to get her daughter back.

Still moving furniture, I decided to go on the road again for a couple of weeks. When it came time to come home, I didn't want to tell Julie. My plan was to surprise her. On Wednesday, I arrived home early in the afternoon. I heard the shower running. It was the middle of the afternoon. She worked in the morning at the restaurant and would have showered in the morning before work. Ashley was not there either. The sheets were draped on the bed, as if two people slept there, and her clothes were lying on the floor.

"Hi, I'm home!" I called out.

"I'm in the shower."

I went and stood by the bathroom door. "You surprised to me see me?"

"Sure am!"

I listened to the running water. "Why are you taking a shower in the middle of the afternoon?"

"I was cleaning and just felt like I needed another shower," she called out.

"Where is Ashley?"

"She spent the night at her aunt's."

"Oh."

I suspected that someone had recently been there, perhaps even stayed the night while I was gone. I asked her, and of course, she denied it. Foolishly, I let it go.

Soon I found out she was going to Crystal Lake often to visit her girlfriends, or so she said. Ashley's father still lived in Crystal Lake. After Julie got Ashley back home, it seemed like the plug was pulled on our relationship and it was going down the tubes. I needed to get out for a while and clear my head. My bike needed some parts, and it was a nice clear day, so I decided to take a ride to the bike shop a few towns away.

When I was in the downtown area where the motorcycle shop was, I saw this beautiful brunette with long silky hair walking down the sidewalk. There was something about this woman that was alluring. I gunned the bike, and she looked up to see where all that noise was coming from. I was just passing her as she looked up and smiled. I pointed at the seat and she shook her head no.

I drove around the block again and pulled up alongside her. "Hi. Want to go for a ride?" I said.

She shook her head. "No, thank you."

"C'mon." I motioned to the seat. "Let's just go around the block."

She hesitated, then shrugged. "All right."

I put out my hand. "I'm Rob."

She shook my hand. "I'm Veronica," she said.

Veronica was a gorgeous petite brunette with the body of a model. She had wavy, silky, dark hair down just past her shoulder blades.

We rode around for a bit, and then I asked her where I could drop her.

"Back by the bike shop," she said.

"Seriously?"

She giggled. "Well, not at the bike shop, but a block away."

"What's there?"

"My apartment."

"Seriously? You live a block from the bike shop?"

"I can prove it to you," she said with a little mischief in her voice.

"Is that an invitation?"

"Would you like it to be?"

"Yeah, that would be great!" I said.

We went up to her apartment, which was above some stores on the main street in town. The place didn't look lived in. There weren't a lot of pictures on the walls, and she only had a few pieces of furniture. But on one of the few chairs was a friend of hers with a little child.

"This is my friend Beth," said Veronica. "And this is my daughter, Story."

"Hi, Beth and Story," I said. I gave the little girl a smile, and she smiled back. After my experience with Ashley, I felt more comfortable around small children. I even knew I could have a rapport with them.

Beth soon took off, and Story went down for a nap, so Veronica and I ended up talking for a little while. She was somewhat of a mystery to me. She had gotten out of a terrible relationship with Story's father, which really hurt her daughter. I thought of Ashley again, and immediately my heart went out to Story.

Veronica had an easy way about her. Even for the short time we were talking, I got the feeling she and I had known each other for years. Finally it was time for me to go, but I really enjoyed my time with Veronica, and I wanted to end it with Julie.

Several days later, Veronica and I met again and had another great time together. She was extremely beautiful and really down to earth. Her daughter took a liking to me as well. She just needed someone to care for her and show her some love. After being with Veronica this second time, I decided I wanted to be with her and not Julie.

I was honest with Veronica and told her that I was seeing someone else but that I was going to end it. Julie was cheating on me. I knew it and wanted to leave her. Veronica didn't seem to believe I was sincere. She got it in her head that I was cheating on Julie and that I was just using her. I tried to explain that wasn't the case, but Veronica didn't buy it. She was not as concerned about herself as she was for her little girl. Story had become very attached to me in just a short amount of time.

Julie must have picked up on something. When she thought she was going to lose me, she laid it on thick, and I fell for it. She told me how much she cared about me and loved me and how glad she was that we were together. This got me thinking. I had a lot of time invested in this relationship, and then there was all I did to get Ashley back, and she was attached to me too. I think I stayed more for Ashley than I did for Julie. I wanted Veronica and felt a deeper connection with her, but that seemed to be over.

I didn't call Veronica, and I'm certain she was wondering where I was as time passed.

At the end of that week, I was having deep regrets about the decision I had made and changed my mind about Julie. The same day, Julie told me she was moving out and going back to Ashley's father.

I couldn't believe it. She'd ruined her relationship with me, and she'd stood in the way of my relationship with Veronica. Immediately after she left, I tried calling Veronica numerous times. I decided to take a ride and talk to her. The landlord said she had just moved out. I was in shock. I couldn't believe she'd gone. I located Veronica's friend, Beth, who'd been over that first day I'd been there.

"She left!" she said, standing in the doorway of her place, not showing any sign of wanting me to come inside. "You hurt her and Story. Veronica was very upset! You knew they just got out of an abusive relationship and they were hurting, and you just hurt them more."

I grabbed both sides of the doorframe and bowed my head. "Beth, it was not my intention to hurt them, I assure you. I really liked Veronica and Story. We all hit it off great. What would I be doing here now if I didn't care about them?"

"Rob, I'm just telling you what she said, okay?"

I took a step back and held up my hands in surrender. "I know that. I know that. But I'm just saying, I really care about her and the little girl. They mean something to me. Truly."

Beth sighed. "Look, you do seem like a nice guy. And I believe you're sincere. But I don't even know where they are, okay? She just left. They disappeared."

I tilted my head. "Come on, Beth, I really need to talk to her. How can I get in touch with her? You've got to help me!"

"Rob, I don't know. I told you. Look, if she calls me, I'll tell her you were here looking for her and you want to talk to her."

"You promise?"

"Yes."

"And will you tell her you believe I'm sincere?"

She smirked. "Yes, I'll tell her. Look, I don't even know if I'll be speaking with her, but I'll tell her you seem sincere."

I thanked her profusely, and then, reluctantly, I left. I couldn't believe Veronica could have disappeared after only a week. How could I let that woman go for Julie? I waited and waited, but Veronica never called. We only knew each other for a short time, but she seemed to really have fallen for me. I ran into Beth again, and she said she finally did talk to Veronica, but Veronica never called me. According to Beth, Story was really missing me. If I'd only known how Veronica really felt about me, I would have definitely left Julie when I got back instead of hanging around in a nowhere relationship.

I let a woman I had strong feelings for slip away. But I didn't just lose one woman, I lost two. Although with Julie, I knew I was going to lose her. She was headed nowhere. I'd already been to nowhere, and I didn't want to go back.

CHAPTER **33**

Cool Bikes
Hot Girls

Time passed, and I was ready for a good year. I thought things had to get better—that they couldn't get any worse. Several months had passed since New Year's, and it dawned on me that this was *the* year—1984. Some intuition or thought I'd picked up seven or so years earlier made me believe this year was going to bring remarkable, positive change into my life. I remember thinking years earlier that if I could only hold on until 1984, something would change. As if my life would make a monumental transition for the better.

A few years ago I read George Orwell's novel *1984*. I was quite amazed by it because it seemed to describe what was happening to society in some respects. The people basically became programmed by the powers that be and followed instructions without ever questioning what they were told. Maybe the events of my life were trying to lead me to the book and not the year. Maybe the hardships and adversity I went through were intended to make me think and ask questions instead of just following the status quo.

I moved back home to my mom's again. Change was in order. I wanted to quit breaking my back with the moving job and start bartending, so my mother got me a job at the Chinese restaurant where she worked. The service bar was the best place for me to start. There was no real pressure and plenty of time to learn. After a couple of months there, I got more comfortable and confident and sharpened my skills. With a little experience under my belt, I started looking for another bartending job. One that had more action. I wanted more money than I was making at the Chinese place. I found a job at a local hotel starting as a server in the restaurant, called Filly's because it was close to Arlington Park race track. The understanding was that I'd start bartending after I was familiar with the restaurant part of the business.

One of the other people working in the restaurant was a lady in her fifties named Eileen. She took to me right away and nurtured me, kind of like a surrogate mother. She always watched out for me and taught me the dos and don'ts of the business. Some of the younger ladies there were very nice and attractive. Eileen thought that Karen and I would make an "adorable couple." She invited Karen and me to her house for dinner.

I was intimidated by the idea of going out with Karen. She wasn't like any other girl I'd gone out with before. Veronica was the closest to Karen, but Karen was not only beautiful, classy, and charming, she also had a good upbringing and came from money—lots of it. She was about nineteen or twenty.

Prior to this night, I'd only admired women like this from afar. Karen was glamorous, in terrific shape, and made a point to stay that way. Karen's stunning looks and personality took her all the way to third place in Miss Illinois.

Eileen and her husband lived in a modest but very nice home in a quiet neighborhood. Everything was very well kept. They had pictures of family on the walls, figurines in a curio cabinet, and an upright piano against one wall. But what really made the house a home was that after thirty-five years of marriage, they were still the cutest couple. Their love and respect for one another was obvious. This was something I'd never seen with my parents. Her husband owned a body shop and didn't seem like the type to help in the kitchen. But after dinner, Eileen and Jack started cleaning up and doing the dishes together. Eileen encouraged us to relax and talk until they were finished.

Karen and I seemed to be getting along well, and then she wanted to go out drinking at a local bar and dance club down the street from my home.

"Uh, we could do that," I said hesitantly. "But you're underage. I can't guarantee I'll be able to get you in."

She giggled. "Don't worry about me getting in, silly."

Damned if she wasn't right. Getting in was no problem for her. It looked to me like the doorman was intimidated by her striking looks and didn't want to card her.

As we made our way inside to find a place to sit, every man in the bar had his eyes locked on Karen. They turned their heads and followed her like they were following the ball carrier in a football game. I even noticed some of the woman briefly checking her out, comparing themselves to her, running through their internal checklists.

Noticing all these men looking at Karen made me feel extremely uncomfortable, even inadequate. She could have had any one of them. And although I was the one on a date with her, I felt like I didn't deserve to be with her. She seemed to have no problem at all with all the admiration she was receiving. She appeared quite comfortable with it; she knew who she was.

At her insistence, we sat at a bar table in full view of the room. Karen order a screwdriver and finished it in two minutes. Then she ordered another. When "Caribbean Queen" came over the sound system, Karen lit up. She said she had to move to that song, and she dragged me out onto the dance floor. When we got back to the table, she ordered another screwdriver. Then another. She must have put seven or eight screwdrivers away in about an hour and a half.

I didn't know how to stop her. Before I could really get my bearings on how this was happening, she was wasted, and I had to get her out of there. I took her back to my place. She wasn't coherent, and I laid her on the couch downstairs. I took her shoes off and tried making her as comfortable as possible. She was in and out of it.

Karen's mother came the next morning to pick her up. That was the last I ever saw or heard from Karen. I didn't want to call her, although I was curious to see if she had any feelings for me. Without a doubt, her mother had made her quit her job and stop any sort of communication with me whatsoever. Her mother must have been pretty disgusted with her, me, or both of us.

So there was failure with another girl. A couple of them seemed out of my hands, but I still didn't like the fact that I got dumped by Julie, and I wanted to get her back. Although it was just for a short time, I'd been like a father to her child. That was more than anyone could say about her biological father. He was nowhere to be found when Ashley was put in a foster home. I felt some redemption was in order. Maybe it was ego driven. In my gut, I wasn't certain she was the one for me. Regardless, I wanted to try and win her back just to see if I could. Did I really want her back?

I hadn't been working out for a couple of months. I wasn't out of shape, but I wanted to get as hard and toned as I could before seeing her. So I hit the weights hard. I tried calling her a few times, and we spoke on occasion, but she was not too interested in coming back to me. That only made me try harder. When it came down to it, I was pretty sure this was not the woman I wanted to spend the rest of my life with anyway.

A couple of months after my one and only date with the runner-up for Miss Illinois, I was finally given the opportunity to start working in the hotel bar and sharpen my skills at making drinks. The bar and restaurant were adjacent to one another. The hostess stand and the bar were separated by a hallway and a door from the lobby. The servers from the hotel restaurant and bar would usually go out dancing and drinking after work. I went out with a couple of the other women at the restaurant. One girl, Denise, was from Las Vegas and had worked as a showgirl. She'd come to Illinois to stay with friends for a much needed break from a nasty divorce she was going through.

After a night of drinking and dancing with her coworker Cindy, a fellow hostess, Denise asked me for a ride home. When I got her back to her place, she invited me up for a nightcap.

"Sorry, Denise," I said. "I gotta be going home."

"Come on, Rob. One drink!"

I shook my head. "Denise, I told you before, I might be a lot of things, but I don't go out with married women."

She scoffed and laughed. "Rob, I'm getting a divorce. I'm separated from my husband. Now, come on."

"That may be, but for now you're still married. When you get your divorce, come see me. I'll be more than happy to go out with you, darlin'. Until then, it's not going to happen. We're just friends, okay? I got to go. See you at work in a couple days."

The next day, like usual, I rode my bike to work, wearing my leather jacket. I didn't wear a helmet, but even on a warm day I always wore my leather jacket as protection. Spilling a bike without one can be brutal. Denise had the day off, so I didn't have to be concerned about seeing her. I kind of liked the fact that she was pushy, but I couldn't date a married woman, and I really didn't want to have that conversation with her over and over again.

I got off work early that day, so I was in a rush to get home, and I forgot to grab my jacket. I headed out on my bike by the same route as always. I was already a few blocks from work when it dawned on me that I'd forgotten my jacket. But I decided to press on and pick it up the next day.

The speed limit was forty-five on the route I normally took home, but I would always push it to about five or ten miles over the speed limit. This was "normal riding speed" for me. Bikes stop quickly, so I was never too concerned about getting a ticket. Riding in the middle of the lane, I was doing about fifty-five. I came to a cross street, and out of the corner of my eye, I caught a policeman parked down the street. I quickly slowed down. I'd been resting my feet on the back passenger pegs, and as soon as I began to move my foot to brake, which I'd done many times before, for some reason my back tire started to fishtail to the right. I was startled, not understanding what has happening. Suddenly everything seemed like it was moving in slow motion. My back end was sliding too far around and seemed to be gliding. I tried to turn into the skid, but I couldn't bring the front end around fast enough. I was now going sideways down the middle of the street. I realized this was it. I was going down!

Amazingly, while I was going down, I noticed two things. First, my speedometer said I was at fifty miles per hour. Second, the cars in my mirror were relatively close behind me. If the crash didn't kill me, it was certain death from being run over by one of the cars. At this point, the back end of the bike was about even with the front. I was sliding forward, the bike started tilting back, and I began to lose my balance. The bike and I were at a forty-five degree angle to the pavement. Then the bike shot out from under me like a bullet and went darting forward on its side. I could hear it crash onto the pavement and the noise of grinding and screeching of metal. And I went down. But I felt like I never hit the pavement. I was sliding on my ass with my arms out to my sides, trying to balance myself and avoid flipping from side to side, and I continued to race forward. I was worried about the cars behind me. Even so, I couldn't worry about them at that moment. I just had to hope they'd seen me fall and would be able to stop in time.

I was trying to keep my balance, keep my head up, and stay on my back. Gradually, I slowed down. With my legs outstretched in front of me, I either put my heels down or my foot got hung up on a small hole in the pavement. Abruptly, like a gymnast, I started tumbling head over heels. After completing the third somersault, I popped up, went slightly airborne a few feet forward, and remarkably landed on my feet. I stood there for a moment, then I staggered like a drunk to the side of the road to get out of the way of any cars. Sirens wailed in the distance.

The policeman I'd seen on the side street had to have seen me go sliding by, and he must have immediately called for an ambulance.

I looked up and saw my bike about seventy-five feet in front of me. I took a quick mental inventory of my body parts, and I seemed to have all my extremities intact, although my arms were bloodied, dirty, and covered with pieces of stones and whatever else I picked up from the pavement. It reminded me of how you take cookie dough and roll it out and then roll it into the candies. Except in this case the candies were dirt, stones, and blood. I noticed my palms on each hand had three divots in them—two divots nearly the size of silver dollars at the top of my hands and one the size of a quarter. Two of the divots had to be at least a quarter of an inch deep. Oddly, they were in the same place on each hand. I could feel the burning in my palms.

My arms had definitely gotten the worst of it. They were also burning. They felt like they were put up against a stone grinder or cheese grater that had shaved off layer after layer of skin. I looked at my legs and saw that my pants looked like they'd gone through a shredder, although my legs seemed okay. They both had mostly minor lacerations. My right leg had one large scrape, but not very deep. Although I couldn't see it, after sliding all that way, surprisingly, my ass didn't seem to feel too bad.

The cop said, "I clocked you going just over fifty before you went down. Usually guys come out of an accident like that on a stretcher. You're actually able to walk away. You're one lucky kid!"

I was still in a daze, but I had enough of my wits about me at the moment to know he was absolutely right. "I know," I said. "I'm not sure how. I can't believe I didn't hit my head. That in itself is remarkable. I don't even know how I fell off my bike. I didn't do anything unusual. The bike just came out from underneath me. That's the strangest thing. I still can't believe my head didn't smack the pavement. I have no bumps or pain on my head whatsoever. Unbelievable! Wow! It felt like I was just smoothly gliding along."

"Look," said the cop, pointing. "The ambulance is here. You better get in, kid."

A paramedic opened the door and helped me get into the ambulance. The driver hit the lights and siren, and off to the hospital we went. The paramedics concurred with the cop. They felt I was incredibly lucky, especially considering how fast I was going.

"A lot of these bikers we bring in that went through what you just did are in the hospital for weeks, if they recover at all. Someone was watching over you today, pal! You should be grateful." He said it with such purpose.

I wasn't sure why, but I was grateful. I felt like I'd been protected. By what and why I don't know, but definitely by something.

Oddly, it was such a smooth and nonviolent accident. It could have been much worse for me than it was. When I arrived at the hospital, they gave me antiseptic and sprayed something on my lacerations to reduce the pain. The nurse took the wrapping off a sanitized scrub brush.

I asked, "What are you going to do with that thing?"

"We have to clean out those wounds," she said. "Get all the dirt and gravel out of there."

I chuckled. "You're joking, right?"

She shook her head. "Nope! This won't hurt too bad. I gave you a little something for the pain."

She was right. It didn't hurt nearly as bad as I thought it would. Incredibly, the X-rays showed no broken bones. I was treated, scrubbed, and bandaged in the emergency room that afternoon, and I was released in the evening. My arms were wrapped with gauze from my shoulders to my hands. I looked like a mummy.

I thought back to my childhood and some of the accidents I'd endured. Many times it had seemed someone was protecting me. I could add this to the list. And considering the way the cop and the paramedics acted, it seemed like this was a biggie. But why? During down times in my life, I often wondered that. I couldn't come up with an answer, but I believed there was one. There had to be. And that belief kept me going, gave me purpose, made me think there was something I needed to become.

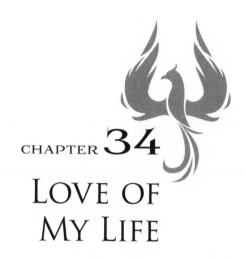

CHAPTER **34**

LOVE OF
MY LIFE

You never know when you're going to meet the love of your life. I'd given up thinking there was anyone in the world for me. I was still dating, but I didn't think anything would ever come of it. Recently, I'd gone out casually with a girl named Lisa, who I'd met at Maxfield's. I was connected to the bar because Matt worked there. He'd been a bartender at the hotel with me, but left bartending to follow his passion. Now he was a DJ at Maxfield's. I envied him. I wasn't even sure I had a passion.

A few days after my accident, my niece had a birthday party. I wanted to go, but I was worried I'd run into my mom there. I didn't want her to see me all bandaged up from the bike wreck. She hated that I rode. But when my sister Robin told me Mom wasn't going to the party, I grabbed Lisa, and we went.

When we showed up at the house, we were mingling with people for a few minutes, and then I rounded the corner into the kitchen and ran straight into my mom. She smiled when she saw my face, but then she frowned when she saw my arms.

"You got in a motorcycle accident, didn't you?" she yelled.

"No, of course not," I said. "I was going through the double doors at work and another server coming from the other side ran into me carrying a tray of hot water from the steam table. The water went flying everywhere and sprayed all over my arms."

"Oh, please," she said.

I rolled my eyes. "Mom, can you just enjoy the party. It's no big deal."

The crazy part was the bandages would be coming off the next day. I knew my arms would still look like crap, but if I'd been wearing a long-sleeved shirt with no bandages underneath, Mom might never have known anything had happened. Sometimes it all comes down to timing.

After I got done dealing with my mom, I had fun at the party. Lisa was great. Everybody liked her, but I knew she wasn't the girl for me. I thought I would never get married.

That following weekend seemed just like any other weekend in July. The bar was crowded with the regulars as well as guests from the hotel. I'd just got done pouring someone a drink and went to the end of the bar and glanced over to look for one of the girls at the hostess stand by the lobby door. She wasn't there, but there was a boy, about ten years old, standing there looking around the room. Next to him was a woman with her back to me. I was about to look away when the woman turned around. And then I couldn't look away. She gave me a feeling like no other woman has in my life—including, surprisingly, Carol. One look at the woman and I said to myself confidently, knowingly, "That's the girl I'm going to marry!"

I can't explain how I knew. Looks had nothing to do with it. There was a definite spiritual connection between us. I felt as if I recognized her. I recognized her spirit. It was like she was a soul mate from a past life. It was as if I found my soul mate. I can't describe it any other way.

I just had one reservation—the little boy. The previous woman in my life had a child, and I didn't want to be the parent to another kid.

I asked her from behind the bar. "Hi, may I help you?" I said.

"Oh, someone's already helping me," she said. "I'm just waiting on some milk for my nephew."

I smiled. "Oh, okay. This is your nephew?"

She was very attractive, about five seven and 125 pounds, with green eyes, a very nice body, and bleach-blonde hair cut straight across above the shoulders. She seemed down-to-earth, confident, and somewhat sophisticated.

Unfortunately, I got distracted by customers, and the next time I looked for her, she was gone. About a half hour later she pulled up a stool at the bar and said hi.

"You're back," I said, surprised. "I'm Rob. I'm glad you came back."

"I'm Lynn. I'm glad I came back too."

I put a napkin down on the bar in front of her. "What'll you have?"

"Make it a pinot grigio."

She stayed at the bar for an hour or so, and I chatted with her between serving drinks. While I was dealing with a few customers in a row, I noticed a guy trying to hit on her, so I just watched to see how she would react. She was obviously trying to give him the brush off, but he wasn't taking the hint, so I stepped in to help out.

"Your friends over there," I said to him as I nodded to a table across the floor. "They were wondering where you'd wandered off to. Why don't you see what they want?"

The guy wandered off with a shrug, and Lynn smiled at me. "Thanks," she said.

"Just part of my job," I said.

We talked for a few more minutes, and before I could ask her, she scribbled something on a bar napkin and handed it to me. "Here's my phone number. Please give me a call."

Later that week, I called Lynn. "I have to work tonight, but did you want to get together when I got off?"

"What time do you get off?"

"About one in the morning. You will probably be sleeping then, won't you?"

"No, no, I'm usually up then. Why don't you come by?"

"You sure?" I wanted to confirm it was okay, especially because she was just back from college and living with her parents in a two-bedroom apartment.

Lynn and her parents lived on the first floor. She told me to come to the patio door and knock quietly so I didn't wake her parents.

I headed over to her place directly from work. I'd sold what was left of my old bike for parts and bought a new one a couple of months later. It was a 1976 Kawasaki 900 LTD. It was a warm summer night, and there wasn't a cloud in the sky. I was enthralled at the prospect of seeing her, and I couldn't help opening up the bike as I made my way to her. But when I turned into her block, I throttled way back and shifted into first to try to keep the roar of my bike low.

I arrived at her patio door about 1:30. She invited me in and we sat on her couch talking for about an hour or so. She had just graduated from college with a degree in administrative justice, but she was currently working as a counselor for troubled kids, which made me think she might be the perfect person for me.

She seemed to have had a good, solid, uneventful, upbringing. She had nice parents and a decent family. It was just the opposite of what I had. Even though I could adapt to different situations, I was afraid she'd think I was a little too rough around the edges for her. Unless she asked, I was not going to reveal anything about my past, but I wanted to know as much about hers as possible. I truly felt this was the woman for me. I was going to marry her.

It was getting really late. The time for the first kiss was upon us, and I had in mind that it should be something special—memorable. After all, I'd already decided there was some spiritual connection between us that would bind us for the rest of our lives. But I started to think, how do I make this really special? And then it became some sort of move, and I realized I was just overthinking it. Relax, I told myself. There's a connection between the two of us. It will naturally be something memorable. I turned to her and put my hand on her face, then slid it around to the back of her head and pulled her toward me. We smiled at each other, and then our lips touched. And it was definitely memorable. *I've* never forgotten it.

It was one of the crazy things in my life. After Lynn and I had known each other for a while, in the course of conversation we figured out we'd crossed paths before. She was the woman I'd been staring at in that restaurant in Flagstaff years earlier. How mystical life can be!

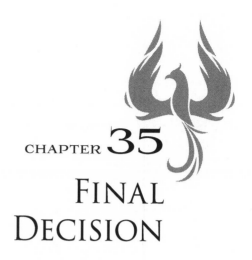

CHAPTER 35

FINAL
DECISION

I couldn't get her out of my head, and I didn't want to. I knew she was the one for me. Lynn and I decided we were going to go out again later that week. Since I only had the bike, when the night came for our second date, I waited for her to come pick me up at my mom's house. The doorbell rang, and when I opened the door, I got a big surprise.

"Hi, Rob. Surprised?"

"Julie? Uh, yeah, I'm definitely surprised." She was dressed in a skimpy top and tight shorts. She'd obviously dressed to impress.

"Honey, I've been doing a lot of thinking, and I decided I want to get back together with you."

"Really?"

She pressed herself up against me, and I stepped away from her, which she took as an invitation to come inside. "Yes, why don't we talk about it? Is that cool with you?" She walked past me and headed for the couch.

"Well I've been seeing someone else for about a week now," I said, still holding the door. "You're a little late."

She turned to me with a frown, still standing. Then the frown became a flirtation smile. "Well, it's only been a week. Come on. We have a lot more time invested with each other than a week. Let's at least talk for a while."

I cocked my head and shook it. "I don't know. Anyway, she's on her way over now. Why don't I call you later?" I pulled the door wider. I was trying not to be too blunt, but I wanted her out of there.

She walked back toward me, but instead of going right out the door, she reached out and stroked my arm. "Okay, Rob," she said in a throaty whisper. "Let's just talk. You can come over to my place tonight, and we will work everything out, okay?"

"I'll call you later," I said, and then I nodded toward the door.

She turned and backed out of the doorway, looking into my eyes with a smile on her face. "That's all I'm asking for," she said.

Her coming back to me was exactly what I'd wanted before Lynn entered into the equation. I had to make this decision between the two, but it wasn't a hard choice. I felt Lynn was a much better woman than Julie would ever be. She'd finished college, which was a good sign she wanted to do something with her life. Julie had already cheated on me. Who knew what she would do in the future? Even if I wanted to get back with her, it would be hard for me to forget about her past behavior. I called Julie later that night and told her I didn't want to get back with her any longer.

CHAPTER **36**

LIE OF MAGNITUDE

The first cloud on the horizon would not appear again for years, but it began here. I'd been dating Lynn for a few weeks. On one of our dates, the subject came up about our previous boyfriends and girlfriends. We were sitting on the couch at my place, just relaxing. I wanted to find out a little bit about her past. I asked her how many guys she'd dated or how many boyfriends she had. Surprisingly, she told me she'd only had one boyfriend, and he left her for another woman.

"I'm glad I met you," she said, setting her beer on the coffee table, "or I would have been an old maid."

I laughed. "Come on," I said. "You're too good looking to be an old maid! You are very attractive. I can't believe you had only one boyfriend."

"Only one. I never went out much."

This conversation would come back to haunt both of us.

When Lynn and I'd been going out for three months, I was ready to ask her to marry me. We got along great and were obviously very attracted to each other. Actually, I was ready when I met her. Or I could have asked her a couple of weeks after I meet her, but I thought for sure she would say no. For her twenty-third birthday, I gave her a giftwrapped ring box. When she first laid her eyes on the box, she seemed panicky. She was talking and laughing nervously. I could tell just by her reaction when I gave her the box she was not ready to get married. She unwrapped the box.

When the paper was off and she slowly opened the box, I said to her, "I thought it's what you wanted."

With a great deal of relief she burst out laughing. "It's your eyebrow hair!"

"Yes, it's what you wanted, wasn't it? You're always playing with it and pulling on it, so I thought you'd like to have it. You were nervous. You thought it was a ring didn't you?"

"I thought it was."

"Okay, well you had your chance. I can take a hint. I won't ask you again."

She shook her head, embarrassed. "That's not it."

"Nope, you had your chance."

We both had a nice laugh over it.

CHAPTER 37

TREK OF
PASSION

I was getting a little older. Maybe I finally started to be more mature. I began wondering what life was all about and where I fit into it. The desire had been brewing and stirring inside of me to do something to help others in a substantial way. Despite the difficult circumstances I'd gone through with Carol, and knowing how much I suffered through it, I started to think about how I could help others who were suffering, too. I wanted to do something, something big, something for many people. I wanted to do something to ease the suffering of others. But what could I do? I had no money, no real support from anyone, and no idea about what to do. I knew one thing—my body was fit and strong. I thought about using my physical strength to help others, but how could I use it? I pondered on this for a week or so. What could I do? I kept asking myself.

Then one night I was watching Johnny Carson. He had a guest on who'd just completed a run across America to help raise awareness and money for a cause he believed in. I could do that, I thought. Only two things were stopping me. I didn't have a favorite charity, and I couldn't run that far. So how could I go about it? I thought maybe I could run, walk, ride a bike, and skate. I didn't recall hearing of anyone doing that. So that's what I decided to do.

But what would be my cause? I'd heard a lot about missing children. Since the kidnapping and brutal death of a young boy just prior to my getting the idea, there was a lot more publicity for missing children. Most of this had to do with the efforts of the boy's father to shed light on this heinous issue—missing and exploited children. I was a runaway. I knew how hard that situation is on the family. And I knew the kind of peril I'd found myself in more than once during that part of my life. A lot of bad things happened to kids who were out on their own and vulnerable. I'd raise money for missing children. I found an organization out of New York that was involved in that issue. I made contact with the director out there and paid for my own flight with the little money I had to learn more about their organization and tour their headquarters. I wanted to make certain the place I was going to raise money for would use the money wisely. The place was well organized but not fancy. That was good. To me it seemed to mean they weren't spending money on themselves but were focused on their mission. I made a commitment to donate all the money I raised to them.

The only problem left to solve was I didn't have the kind of training to pull something like this off. I needed to get into even better shape. I started to build my endurance by riding a bike and jogging. I still lifted weights but lighter amounts and more reps for endurance. I made sure I was eating a lot of calories throughout my training. I didn't really have the money to buy a bike, skates, clothing, and all the supplies I'd need, and I sure didn't have the money to pay for lodging along the way. I also didn't have the money for a trainer.

Still, I approached the goal methodically, taking it step by step. I decided to train myself and figured I could probably be ready within two to three months, if all went well. I couldn't start in the winter or early spring, because there would be too much snow in the Rockies. I didn't want to deal with any more potential hazards than I had to. I'd leave Memorial Day weekend and end right around Labor Day weekend.

I knew mapping the route would be a little tricky, since I wasn't familiar with the lay of the land and I couldn't use Interstates or some major highways. Of course there was no GPS in those days, and no Google Maps, so I bought maps for every state I would travel through and plotted my course. I highlighted the route I'd take through each of those states. I called some towns to find out if there were any local ordinances that would impede my trip. I also asked for advice on where to stay and marked those spots with a highlighter. It's about 3200 miles across the country from start to finish, so that meant that if I went only forty miles a day, I could accomplish this in less than three months. I knew I'd be able to do forty miles a day, no problem.

Just thinking about what happened to me as a runaway and all the suffering I went through motivated me. The kids I was doing this for didn't make the choice to leave home like I did. They were taken against their will. All I needed to think about was those kids and families who were suffering, and that would be more than enough motivation for me to finish this trek and bring awareness for a great cause. I was excited and couldn't wait to get started.

The next issue I had to deal with was housing. Where was I going to stay, and how was I going to transport all my gear? I would probably need a lead/flag car to make other drivers aware of me in order to be safe. That could be my beater of a car, a blue '76 Nova. If I did only forty miles a day, there might not be lodging near me, or I might have to travel far to get to it. I realized what I needed was an RV where I could sleep and store my stuff. But I didn't have one of those or know anyone who did. There just happened to be a RV show in Chicago the following weekend. Nothing was going to stop me. I was doing this for a great cause and wanted to do what I could to help.

Necessity is the mother of invention. I had no idea how to make my goal happen, so I just invented the methods as I went along. I didn't have a professional trainer, but I'd worked out a lot, and I knew how to do that. Still, I felt it would be good to have some motivation, so I teamed up with a friend. In our off hours, we'd go to a local gym. It was clean and nice, but it wasn't a chain or name brand. It had lots of weights and some stationary bikes and other basic equipment. I developed a sort of circuit routine. I wasn't looking to add pounds but wanted to increase my strength and endurance. So I'd go from arms and dumbbell curls to lateral raises to squats to bench presses. Then I'd hit the stationary bike for a sprint, then back to the weights. It was effective, and with the help of my buddy, I could stick with it. The road work I did on my own. I'd just jog or cycle out in the neighborhood. It was a lot of hard work, but I felt good doing it.

When I wasn't training, I took to the phones to drum up support. I tried to contact people who could help me with this trek, including corporate sponsors. I was trying to get anything I could in the way of help, including training gear. I made phone call after phone call. Of course, these were big organizations I was contacting. Just finding the right person to talk to was an arduous task. Many times I felt I was getting the run around. I knew it wasn't intentional. They didn't get calls like mine every day, so how would they know who to direct me to? Still, it was frustrating. I kept a grueling schedule. If I wasn't at my job, almost all my time was spent either training or working the phones.

Finally I found someone at Nike I could talk to. I explained to the lady what I wanted to do and why. She agreed to sponsor me and send me all the training gear and shoes I would need. It was awesome! I had Nike as a sponsor!

On the weekend of the RV show, Lynn and I had to go to the city to check it out. It was at a convention center with a huge cavern of a show-room for big events like this. The place was wall to wall RVs. There were some looky-loos around, but many of the potential customers were people who obviously had money. I didn't look like them. I was afraid I didn't look like a serious customer and wouldn't be taken seriously, but Lynn encouraged me.

"You're *not* the typical customer," she said. "You're much more than that. Tell the dealers what you're doing. They'll take you seriously."

So I just walked up to the first dealer I came to and introduced myself and my project. I hoped maybe they would do the same thing the Nike folks did—sponsor me. I didn't figure they'd give me an RV, but I hoped somebody would let me use one for a few months. Well, the first guy wasn't interested, but he did say he admired what I was doing and wished me luck. A few other people said no, but then I came across a man who worked at a car dealership that also sold RVs. He seemed to be moved by the passion I had for what I was trying to do, and he agreed to talk to the owners and explain my situation to them.

I told him I already had Nike as a sponsor and that I intended to put the logos of all the sponsors on the side of the RV, just like his company. I was so excited that he had agreed to talk to the owners of his company. I think my enthusiasm was contagious. He seemed as excited to help me as I was to do this trek. He told me to give him a call on Monday and he would let me know what the owners would do.

I couldn't wait to call him on Monday morning. When I did, he told me the owners had agreed to lend me a brand new RV to use on my trek.

This was no doubt a miracle. It was destined to happen. He asked if I could come up to his dealership so the owners could meet me, work out some logistics, and discuss what size RV I would need. I couldn't believe this just happened.

What is the process to manifest things? Make a decision, create a clear image in your mind of what you want, and marry that image with an energized emotion. I didn't realize it at the time, but I was following the right process, plus, I believe it was because of my strong determination and desire to see this through that things were falling into place, even as unbelievable and impossible as they seemed.

Since I didn't have any money and thought I might need to fly back to New York to meet with the sponsors, or fly home in case of an emergency, I thought I should try to get an airline to sponsor me. I'd started by opening the phone book and making calls, starting with the *As* and working my way down. I spend hours calling them, and soon realized this was going to be tough. I was on the *Ts* and was running out of airlines to call when I came across TWA. After being transferred and redirected several times, I ended up talking to Michael McAllister in Saint Louis.

Michael had an English accent. After hearing my story, he was gracious and more than willing to help me.

"I'll see what I can do," he said. "I'm not going to promise you anything. Sometimes things take a while around here. I'll call you back as soon as I have some news for you."

Much to my surprise, he called me the following week. I'd just gotten in from running and already had my heart rate up. When I heard his voice, my heartbeat probably went up even more from the suspense of wondering what he would say.

"Rob, this is Michael McAllister from TWA."

"Hi, Michael. Nice to hear from you." I hoped the news he had for me would be nice.

"I have some great news for you. Anywhere you need to fly in the United States, you can fly there free with us."

"Really?" I said. "That's great! Michael I can't thank you enough for getting this done for me."

"It was my pleasure. I'm so glad we can help."

That was so awesome. Without knowing anything about publicity or marketing, I was able to get someone to lend me a brand new RV, get all my clothes and footwear from Nike, and get TWA to fly me anywhere I wanted to go in the US.

Now I needed a bike sponsor. Since I'd gotten so many other big things done, I figured finding a sponsor with a bike wouldn't be too hard. I'd worry about that later.

At that moment, what I really wanted to do was find someone to drive the RV for me. And I figured I might need a few other people to go with me.

I wasn't sure if Lynn could take off work without losing her job, but at least it was a place to start. She agreed to help and was more than happy to do what she could. The next day she explained the situation to her boss and was able to take a leave of absence for a few months. Although it was a lot of work, it was extraordinary how smoothly everything was coming together so that I could carry out this trek.

My training was going well, although I started feeling some discomfort in my right foot, and my hamstring in my left leg had a slight strain in it, but this seemed pretty minor and was not really hindering my training regimen. I continued to train at the gym with one of my motorcycle riding buddies.

I realized the more people I could make aware of my trek, the more it would help the cause, so I decided to go to the newspapers. I contacted a local newspaper and caught the interest of a reporter. She agreed the story was worth her coming out to talk to me.

When she came over, I told her in great detail why I wanted to do this and why I was motivated to do so. I think she could tell I was serious, not just by my enthusiasm, but by the fact that the dining table was completely covered with the maps I was using to plot my route. She was moved by my childlike enthusiasm and my passion to help. She told me she wanted to get some pictures of me training.

She had a photographer meet me at the gym, and one of the photos he took was printed with the article she wrote up.

I figured if I could get a local paper interested, maybe I could get some national attention. I decided to contact Johnny Carson to see if I could get on his show. Well, I guess TV wasn't ready for me yet. After a half dozen calls and letters, I got no callbacks.

By this time, I was a month and a half into training and my foot was becoming more tender. I could feel discomfort every time I came down on it. In addition to the slight strain in my left foot, I also tweaked my hamstring in my right leg. I guessed I'd been pushing a bit too hard to get my training in. I definitely needed to get checked out by a doctor to make certain I wasn't going to injure myself further. I didn't trust many doctors, but I knew there was one I could trust.

There are few people in my life that I can look back on and say they were a good person. Dr. Berg was one of those people. Even though it's been several years since that tragic night of the accident, I was still very grateful to Dr. Berg for putting my leg back together. He seemed to truly care about me despite my bad attitude, wearing my emotions on my sleeve, and acting out occasionally toward others. Certain people always seem to look out for me, which always amazes me.

I made an appointment to see him for an exam. I told him I was training to do a cross country trek to raise money and awareness for a missing children's organization.

"It was because of you, Doc, that I'm able to do this. You put me back together."

He seemed very humbled by my words. He examined my hamstring and took X-rays of my foot.

When he came back into the exam room with my X-rays, he shoved the films up into the clips on the light board. "Rob, I know this is going to disappoint you, but you're going to need to take some time off from training." He pointed to a spot on one of the films.

"What's that?" I said. I knew what it was, but I didn't want to believe it.

"It's a small but significant stress fracture. Not as dramatic as a traumatic fracture but just as serious. And it takes just as much time to heal. It's not the end of the road, but you have to stay off it for now. If you continue to train, it will only get worse. Also, both of your hamstrings need a break for a while too."

I thought about it for a moment and then shook my head. "I don't think that's going to work. I only have a month and a half before my trip starts. I need to continue to train."

"Rob—"

I held up a hand. "Okay, Doc, tell you what. I'll take a couple of days off."

He cocked his head and smirked.

"Listen, thanks for everything. It's great seeing you again. And thanks again for putting me back together after the accident."

He reached out and shook my hand. "The visit is on the house, Rob. But I hope you'll give it more than a couple of days."

"I'll do what I can," I said.

CHAPTER **38**

TRUSTING THE
JOURNEY

I was impatient to go back to working out. This was going to be a life-changing event for me, and I wanted to get back to it as soon as possible. I did take a couple days off, but then I went right back to training. I pushed myself even more than before.

The third morning back into my training routine, I went out running after my weightlifting session. I was dodging a little pothole on the pavement and came down on my foot awkwardly. I could feel the pain shoot straight up my leg, and I tried slowing down, skipping on my left foot as to not come down hard on my right again. I was only able to put a minimum amount of pressure on my foot without feeling a significant sharp pain. I went a few more steps, but then I settled into a slightly limping walk with my hands on my hips, mumbling curses under my breath.

Running was out of the question. I couldn't believe this was happening. I walked home and skipped the rest of my training for the day, thinking I'd start up again the next morning. When the next morning came, my foot was not much better; it was a bit swollen. I tried to do some other activities besides running, hoping it would heal fast.

I thought since I lost time because of my foot I could make it up on the bike. I climbed on and headed out. I was using the ball of my foot, but I could withstand the pain and pedal through it. The pain got progressively worse in my foot, and I continued to aggravate both of my hamstrings. I couldn't stop training; there was too much at stake—too many kids and families to help. And what about all the people who'd helped me, my sponsors? I didn't want to let them down, either. They put a lot on the line to help me. Eventually, I had to face the grim reality. My injuries were too extensive. With less than a month left to train, I couldn't heal enough to make it across the country.

My injuries were painful, but it hurt even more to let the people in New York and my sponsors know that I was not able to go through with my trek. I thought I was really going to make a difference this time. I thought for sure I would be able to help the families and the kids through this trek. I never thought my body would be the thing that would give out. I really let a lot of people down. I felt like I'd failed at what I set out to do, especially since everything had been coming together so smoothly. I took the disappointment very hard. I had to struggle to get over it. I'm not sure I ever really did. At the time this seemed typical of my life. No matter how hard I tried, I seemed to be programmed to fail.

Lynn was very supportive and sympathetic about the whole thing. When I finally resigned myself to the fact that the trek wasn't going to happen, we sat on the couch together and she just let me unload a lot of feelings I had about it, about my failures in life, and where that all came from. Inevitably, of course, I got around to telling her the story of my mom's attempt to kill me. It was a pretty heavy conversation, for sure. And I was so grateful to have Lynn, a woman I could really trust and rely on.

To cheer me up after all that, Lynn said she was going to take me downtown to a nice restaurant. It sounded nice, but for some reason, I started to feel really uncomfortable about it. It hit me that talking about my mom might have triggered my anxiety over going to special events. We ended up staying in that night.

CHAPTER 39

OPPORTUNITIES

Andrea, a friend of my mother's, came over one night because she wanted to share a business opportunity with my mother. Mom suggested I come down to listen as well. I wasn't really interested. I enjoyed bartending, riding my bike, and partying, but I realized I couldn't live like that forever.

Working as a bartender was getting old and I couldn't support a family this way, so perhaps it was a time for a change. With a skeptical but hopeful mind, I listened to what Andrea had to say. In the days that followed, I thought about this opportunity, and the more I thought, the more sense it made to me. It required me to get a license to sell life insurance, which I could easily study for in my spare time. I started going to trainings at Andrea's office, which was about an hour drive from my house.

In the meantime, Lynn and I decided to live together. We found a place not too far from her parents and my mother. It was a very small, one-bedroom apartment. The neighbor above us was a night owl, and it almost sounded like there was an open door from our place to his. We could hear every move he made, and we became intimately familiar with his favorite music. Even after trying to talk to him calmly, he had no respect and continued with his rude behavior. We decided to move after living there for only two months. We found a much more spacious place to live, with an underground garage. And the landlord was cool.

CHAPTER **40**

A DIFFERENT PATH

One Saturday morning in December 1986, I headed down to the office for some training with Andrea. "Did you see those houses off of I-88?" I asked as soon as I walked in. "They're really nice. I'd like to live here."

She frowned and shook her head. "Robert, you don't want to live in this area. Those houses look nice, but there's too much pollution from the airport."

I pictured the airport and all the planes taking off and landing and all the fumes they gave off. "Yeah, I guess you're right."

"Hey, sit down for a second, Robert," she said. "I want to talk to you about something."

"Okay," I said, settling into the couch. "What's up?"

She sat on the edge of the desk. "Well, I wasn't going to tell you about this because you didn't seem like the person that would be interested. But I am going to tell you anyway. There's a place I want to bring you to."

"What kind of place?"

"It's a spiritual place. It's something pretty remarkable. My husband, Frank, who's a doctor, and I have been practicing it for a few months now. Are you a spiritual person?"

"No, not really. The last time I went to church was on Christmas a few years ago. And the only reason I went then was because my mother asked me to go. I just did it to make her happy. Religion doesn't make sense to me. There's just too much contradiction. Everyone says their way is the right way, and if you don't believe what they believe, you're going to hell."

There are so many religious beliefs in the world, and there are good people in all of them. People who lead good, happy lives. It wasn't until much later in my life, but eventually I came to believe that, for me at least, spirituality was an individual quest and that understanding consciousness was vitally important. I've made it an essential aspect of my life. But I had to go through quite a journey to get to that point.

When I'd been in my teens, I didn't really see a need for religion in my life. When I was sixteen, a preacher had come to my door. He was starting a new church. I asked him how I could be saved. He told me to read something out of the Bible. I read the verses he recommended, but afterward, I told him I didn't feel saved. Even though I didn't feel it, he assured me I was saved.

If someone saved me from drowning, that would be tangible. I'd have been able to feel it. I would have experienced it. Maybe he meant when I died I'd be saved. Then my question was, how did he know with 100 percent certainty, and what actual proof did he have that I'd be saved?

But he didn't have any proof. None. I know people have had near-death experiences, but that's what they are—near death, not death. In actual death, no one came back five months later and said, "Holy cow, you won't believe what's going on up there." Religion never made sense to me; it only seemed like it wanted to control me. And those big, dimly lit churches always seemed to have a negative vibe. They gave me the creeps. I felt religion had failed me.

At the time, Lynn and I thought what Andrea told us about made more sense than mainstream religion, so we decided to join the organization. I wound up having an extremely active role in it over the years, including responsibilities on the national level. Before I became a member I remember being at the center one day and a tear rolled down my cheek. I asked someone why that happened. They told me my soul was happy. I didn't feel happy. In any case, it was an interesting phenomenon. To a certain degree, despite its own limitations, this organization expanded my vision and got me to think more broadly, focusing on thoughts like gratitude, love, humbleness, and introducing me to this world of spiritualism, even though their version is skewed and limiting. It was quite a long introduction. I felt I had reached a ceiling long ago and wasn't improving, but it took more than twenty years for me to begin to snap out of it and start looking into other things to help me improve, which opened my eyes to the narrow beliefs I'd held in the organization. After nearly three decades, I finally left. Honestly, I was a little afraid to leave for fear of what would happen to me if I did. Would I die? Because I was a sinner, I was constantly told I had to work on eliminating my karma. When I was going through a very difficult time, a senior staff member counseled me, but he didn't teach me how to create a new reality (or figure out ideas for how I could change my situation). Frankly, he had no idea how to do it, nor were any of their teachings about creating a new reality, only apologizing for our karma/sins and offering service to compensate. He told me that I might have to live this way the rest of my lifetime. I felt a sense of aloneness and hopelessness, but at the same time something inside said this is bullshit. There is always a way out! That's one thing I did learn.

Another senior member told me I might die if I left. Now that's fear and control in action. Not surprisingly, talking to former members at the time, they'd had the same feelings when they left but were now leading happy, productive lives. Of course, if I knew then what I know now, I'd have left much earlier. But I have no regrets. Whatever was right or wrong about that place, it was what I needed at the time. The majority of people will (like I did) just follow without questioning what they're taught by their parents, authority figures, or someone they trust.

What I'm about to say may be extremely difficult for some to understand, but in some respects, I don't regret that nearly fatal day in April when I was eleven. Bizarre, right? But the gift I received, other than a new lease on life, was the ability to question and think for myself instead of being a blind follower. It made me look at life in a different light than most people. That said, what makes me feel worse in some respects and what's bizarre to me is when I see people following any particular religion because someone else did it before them. They don't seem to be questioning its validity in their own lives. Isn't religion supposed to solve suffering and make people happy? Then why are so many people still suffering in this world? I stayed with this religious organization for a good while, but in the end, my sense of independence led me to question what their teachings were all about, and I was able to go my own way.

I'm grateful I was able to be open and have the courage to question my own belief system, not only about religion, but about all things in my life. If you're not happy or feeling good, it's because you're not thinking good. If you're not thinking good, that means your thoughts are in conflict with your beliefs. To overcome this you may want to closely examine your belief system because something is not in harmony. I understand why people don't do it, because it may shatter their belief systems. It shattered mine. Well, I don't mind being different. I'd rather know a higher level of truth than continue to live a lie. You see the futile efforts of those who scream for change, but you realize they're only addressing a symptom not the cause. When you know the truth the world starts making more sense in its own perverted way. My suffering subsided and even ended when my awakening began. I learned that this life and religion wasn't what I thought it was. This wasn't some hypothesis I formed; these were facts.

I realized when I gave up my power and put it in something outside of me that I was giving someone the right to tell me what to think and what to believe, making me virtually powerless—a sheepish follower. Herein lies the control.

To me, the world of God—let's just call it Source—seemed to be one without boundaries, which religions wanted to build around me to confine me to a certain dogma. When I go through challenging times now, I go within and connect with the Source, the universal consciousness. My suffering started to end when I awakened to this truth, when I realized that Source is within me, that I am Source. I certainly did not need to give my power away and rely on something outside of me. I believe this only prolonged my suffering.

If you or your kids ever played with Playdoh, you know you can tear off a piece, roll it out, then make a stick man, stars, animals, etc. What becomes of the Playdoh? Is it a stick man, a star, or an animal? For a short time it is, but it never loses its essence, which is Playdoh. When you're done playing, it returns to the source of the Playdoh. Our existence, in a nutshell, is similar to the Playdoh. We come from Source to this three-dimensional world. We have experiences, then when we leave this three-dimensional realm we will return to Source. Therefore, you're part Source. It's that simple. It took a while (like I said, I'm a slow learner), but I came to realize I never had to look outside of myself for this power. It's always been, and will always be, within me—never outside of me.

Later I realized the tear I shed that day in the center wasn't from happiness. I believe my soul was telling me something just the opposite, but again, I wasn't awake to answer the call from my higher self.

CHAPTER **41**

ENGAGEMENT

L ynn and I had been dating for a year and half. From the moment I laid my eyes on her, I knew she was the girl I was going to marry. It was finally time to make the commitment to her and ask her to marry me. The first time I gave her a ring box, as a joke, I knew she wasn't ready to marry and that she'd be relieved it was just a joke. But we'd grown a lot in our relationship, and I knew we were both ready. I'd been able to save some money. Lynn liked amethyst, so I picked out a pear-shaped amethyst engagement ring with two small diamonds on either side.

I've never really been a traditionalist, but I thought about what it would be like to ask her father first if I could marry his daughter. Charlie was a little quiet and really didn't express himself. I didn't have an answer for his inevitable question: "How are you going to support my daughter?" So I decided to ask Lynn directly, without getting her father's permission. It was Valentine's Day, and we had plans to go out to dinner. Before we went out, I took her into the living room.

"Have a seat on the couch," I said. "I have some champagne in the fridge. I'll get it."

In the kitchen, I uncorked the bottle of champagne and grabbed a couple of glasses. With the ring in my pocket, I sat on the couch next to her. I poured her a glass of champagne, then poured mine. With my glass in my right hand, I put my left arm around her and began to tell her what she meant to me. She started to tear up. Valentine's Day, champagne—she knew what was coming next.

I told her how much I loved her and how much she meant to me. I told her how much my life had changed since I'd met her. Then I asked the big question.

With tears rolling down her face, overjoyed, she cried, "Yes! I knew you were going to ask me!"

"I'm sure for at least a split second you might have thought there was another eyebrow in that box, didn't you?" I said.

We both laughed. I was very happy. After all I'd been through, I was allowed to find my true soul mate.

CHAPTER 42

THE TURNING
POINT

I was becoming a different person. I started to think of myself as a success, not as a failure. I had thought of myself as a failure for so long that I now had to come up with a different self-image. I was the successful person where everything was going right.

One day, when Lynn and I were in the kitchen fixing dinner together, I stopped her from what she was doing and turned her toward me. "You notice anything different about me?"

She looked at my shirt, my hair, my face. She seemed bewildered.

"Nothing crazy has been happening to me lately," I said. "Trouble doesn't seem to be following me around like it used to."

She smiled. "Now that you mentioned it, yeah, you're right. What do you think that's from? Do you think it's from changing your thoughts?"

The people in the religious organization said our lives would change; I didn't think they meant like this. Suddenly nobody was coming up to me wanting to fight me or arm wrestle. There were no outbursts of anger. I even seemed to be getting along well with my dad. This was remarkable. I don't know how else to explain it. Change your thoughts; change your life.

CHAPTER 43

THE FLOOD

Lynn and I were engaged six months, then we were to be married in August of 1987. Two weeks prior to our wedding, there were torrential rains in our area with rainfall totals the highest in some hundred years. There was a creek behind our building that overflowed its banks and started creeping toward our building. The water rose rather quickly. I woke up on the third morning of the rains and looked out the living room window. I saw the low, dark gray sky with the rain still pouring down in buckets.

A lot of cars were pulling out of the garage. Because I worked odd hours, I hadn't seen the morning routine of the building before. I turned to Lynn. "I never realized that everyone left for work around the same time."

When I looked out the window again, I saw someone drive his car onto the dry part of the grass next to a little berm. It finally dawned on me that these people weren't going to work. They were getting their cars from the underground garage because it was starting to fill up with water.

Just then, I heard a pounding on the door, and someone screamed from the other side, "Move your cars! Move your cars!"

I looked at Lynn and grabbed my shoes and ran downstairs to move our car. The water was a couple of inches deep already in this massive garage, which was about two football fields long.

I moved our car, but I was still uncertain that the water would be able to flood this garage. As I was walking back to my apartment, our neighbor asked, "Should I move my car?"

"I'm not sure," I said. "We did it just in case."

She'd lived there a lot longer than Lynn and I had, so I figured she'd know more about the potential flooding of the garage than I would. Apparently, she decided to leave her car in the garage.

A couple of hours into it, we'd all resigned ourselves to the fact that nobody was going to work that day. One of my neighbors had Lynn and me over for Bloody Marys.

We had a drink and started playing cards while waiting for the rain to subside, but it just kept coming down. Periodically, we would look out the window to check on the rising water. We noticed it seemed to be rising a little quicker, so we decide to go outside for a look. We walked down the stairs and looked into the basement first.

When we opened the front door to the building, we were surprised that the water had risen halfway up the front stairs. Outside, we observed that water was pouring into the garage. We could still see cars that were in there. A brand new Cadillac had been left on the entrance of the ramp of the garage. We watched water roll over the roof of the car, and it soon disappeared. As the water was rising rather swiftly, we went back inside our apartment. On the first floor, we noticed the carpet was a little damp. The water had now begun to seep into the first floor. Fortunately for us, we lived on the third floor, and there was no threat of the water rising that high.

After we got back upstairs, we noticed the water seemed to be rising even faster than before. The road in front of our building quickly became a stream. Later that afternoon it looked like a raging river had replaced the stream. The water looked only one to two feet deep, but it was moving very rapidly. The fire department rescue squad was able to navigate their way to our complex to help those who would have a difficult time crossing the water. They loaded them onto a boat and got them to dry land. One of the firemen, dressed in his waterproof suit, was enjoying himself as he allowed the water to carry him down river on his back until he was able to reach the next building.

As for the rest of us, the fire department told us that the building would need to be evacuated because it was no longer safe or sanitary. This put a little crimp in our wedding preparations. The only thing we could do was move back to our parents' homes until our wedding. So Lynn moved back with her parents. I once again moved back to my mom's house, which I thought would never happen again. My dad, for some reason, wasn't coming to my wedding. He used my mother as an excuse, but he was only thinking about himself. My grandfather wasn't going to show up either. This was very disappointing and hurtful to me.

A few weeks before our wedding, my dad had a party for Lynn and me to celebrate our marriage. Much to my surprise, my grandfather popped out from one of the rooms as a surprise for me. I was very happy to see him, since I hadn't seen him in some time.

"What are you doing here?" I said.

He wasn't one for showing any emotion. He just mumbled something, and I gave him a big hug.

CHAPTER **44**

WEDDING

We had a small wedding of approximately of eighty people. Honestly, I have to say it was one of the dullest weddings I'd ever been too. After being married for a short time, we moved across the courtyard to a two bedroom apartment in the complex where we'd been living. The insurance sales had slowed, and with the new place I needed to make sure I kept the money flowing, so I picked up some hours driving a limo. That turned out to be a good job because the income was immediate.

I'd been trying to transform my attitude and practice these newly discovered principles, and I noticed a remarkable change in my life in just a short time. Not only was I not getting static from people I encountered, but my health dramatically improved.

Over the first couple of years of my spiritual practice, the biggest transformation took place. I noticed these changes that occurred have seemed to make my life more fulfilling and peaceful. It was the first step on my road to a new life.

CHAPTER 45

THE POWER OF CONSTRUCTIVE THOUGHTS

The power of the mind is mysterious, but at the time I didn't realize I could harness that power. I would soon come to find out that I could change my life with positive thoughts, and I would prove it to myself in a really big way. There was a new paper and supply store near our apartment, which we occasionally visited. To promote their new store, they were raffling off a numerous prizes including a grill and a brand new Jeep Comanche pickup truck. Since I'd been driving the limo, we had only one car for a while. This was fine because the limo company allowed me to drive the limo home and borrow it for personal use as well. I filled out a couple of entry forms while I was in the paper store, thinking it would be nice to win the grill, not even considering to win the truck. On our way out, I grabbed a few other entry forms to fill out and bring back on our next trip.

I'd never won anything, but since you could enter as many times as you wanted and the drawing was a couple months out, I figured I had a pretty good chance to win if I kept filling out entry forms. So I filled them out, dropped them off next time I went by, and picked up some more. I started to think if I filled out enough, I might even have a shot at winning the truck. Soon I became obsessed with winning the truck. I pictured the truck being mine, then I felt with an energized emotion that it was mine and that I was happy because I owned it. I didn't realize at the time that this is the very process to follow in order to manifest things into reality.

I frequently told my wife I was going to win that truck. She thought I was crazy and would just roll her eyes. One day when I visited the store, I took a good look at the truck. I wanted to sit in it and get the real feel of it, but the door was locked. I noticed it was a stick shift with no air conditioning or radio. I thought I wouldn't mind no AC. I'd just putting a sliding window in the back. I'd have plenty of ventilation. And I could have a stereo installed, no problem. This would be a great little truck for me.

Time went on and eventually I thought the date had passed for the drawing. I was disappointed. I'd put so much energy into picturing the truck as mine that I really felt like I was going to win it. It was one of those oh-well moments.

We invited my dad and his wife, Shirley, over for dinner and to play cards one night. As we were deep into a game of Hearts, the phone rang.

I answered.

"Is this Robert?" the voice on the other end asked.

"Yes," I said. "Who's this?"

"This is the manger over at the Avery paper and supply store. You entered our raffle?"

"Yes, I did." At this point I thought he was going to tell me I just won the smoker grill I wanted, because I knew the truck had been raffled off already.

He said, "Well I got great news for you, Robert. You won the raffle for the truck!"

"What?" I honestly thought I'd misheard him.

"You won the truck!"

I covered the phone and turned to everyone. "I won the *truck*!" I shouted.

The manager said, "You sure entered a lot of times, didn't you?"

"I sure did, and my wife thought I was crazy for doing it. I just felt like I was going to win that truck. It felt like it was mine!"

Lynn couldn't believe I won the truck. But I did.

Not long after that, we moved to another apartment complex a few towns away. We'd found an inexpensive place because we were trying to save enough money to make a down payment for a house. Four years later we bought our first house, a townhouse in Streamwood, Illinois. That was in 1993, just a few months before our first child was to be born. We made the decision that she would quit work after having the baby so that someone would always be home with our children. We knew this was going to be a sacrifice financially, but it would be worth it to have a stable environment for our new family.

Things seemed to be going great at the new place, but after living there a year, our mortgage company told us they'd made a mistake with our escrow taxes. This caused our mortgage payment to go up by over $400 a month. About the same time, my insurance sales job was not working out so well, and we started falling behind on our mortgage to the point that our home was in pre-foreclosure. During the time we were living in our first home, our family grew from one child to four, and we had home births in that townhouse for all four children.

Our home was in and out of foreclosure for the next eight and a half years. Though these were very stressful times, on a couple of different occasions we would receive some relief when mystery gifts would show up at Christmastime for our kids. Even when we sold our home, much to our surprise we were allowed to get some money back to help us find and rent a new place. I thought our financial problems were a thing of the past. Unfortunately, they were about to become more intense.

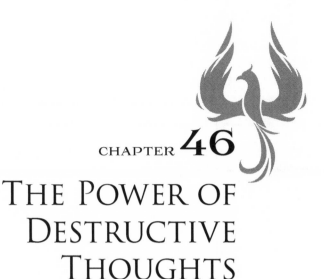

CHAPTER **46**

THE POWER OF DESTRUCTIVE THOUGHTS

When I was younger and trying to find my way, the computer revolution was just starting. My father told me to get involved in computers, and I investigated it for a while, but I wasn't much into school. I went to look at a technical school where I could complete a two-year program in computers, but they still wanted me to take English and other studies that had nothing to do with computers. This turned me off tremendously. I didn't know why I needed English when I want to learn about computers.

That was another big mistake on my part—not recognizing my paradigms. Of course, looking back I can see that the signs of failure were quite evident; I just couldn't see them at the time. I should have applied myself, regardless of the requirements for English and other classes. They probably would have benefitted me. I saw it as a matter of importance and a matter of principle, so I decided not to go. Oh, if I could start over again!

Ironically the company where my dad had worked for the last twenty years was going through a lot of changes. The owner retired, and his son took over the business. New technologies were coming into the workplace. Skilled labor was being replaced with computers. My dad was fifty-eight at the time. At that age, he knew it would be very difficult to find new work. This seemed like the growing trend in America—fire the older, more experienced, larger salary employees, and replace them with younger inexpensive labor or technology. My dad took this very hard and personally. He'd given his blood, sweat, and tears to that company, and he was always the one the company could count on for completing a difficult job and getting it done on time.

My dad tried finding new work, but he was turned down everywhere he went. His health started to deteriorate, and he started getting tremors and feeling more insecure about himself. His wife was continuing to work, and they had enough money to live and retire on, but for some reason he could not get past losing his job. The more time went by, the more he resented being fired. It was almost like he felt they had a vendetta against him. He didn't know where else to turn or what to do anymore. Life had given him something he couldn't deal with. No matter how handy or skilled he was in the material sense, he was lacking the spiritual understanding and the mind power he needed to make it through this low point in his life.

One day it had snowed about ten inches, so I went over to Dad's place with my two-year-old daughter, Brianne, to see if he'd dug himself out. He was happy to see me and the only grandchild he ever knew. To my surprise the snow still covered the driveway. While I was plowing the driveway, I saw my little girl looking out the door with her grandfather behind her. They both turned and closed the door. That little girl brightened some days for my father. I always knew that deep down my father had great love for all of his kids, and if he had it to do it all over, he wouldn't make the same mistakes he did in this life with his own children.

After the drive was plowed, we continued to hang out for awhile, and I let him spend time with his granddaughter. That always seemed to cheer him up. That was the last time I would see my dad alive. He passed away five weeks before his second granddaughter was born. I was by his side when he died, along with my stepmother and stepsister. My grandfather followed him nearly two years later, and I was by his side as well.

CHAPTER **47**

ARRANGED MEETING

Since I was the director of the youth for the religious organization for Chicago and also the entire North American region, I was to attend a conference in New York, but I had no desire to participate. My ego got the best of me, and I felt I already had the training I needed and that I was not going to learn anything new, so it wouldn't be a good use of time and money.

I'd only been in New York briefly, back when I was planning my trek across the country, so I thought I'd go to the training but focus on experiencing the city and taking in some sites. I unenthusiastically went on Labor Day weekend in 2001—one week before 9/11.

When the plane was loading, I could see it wasn't a full flight, so I hoped no one would be sitting next to me. I just needed some peace and quiet on the way there. With my nose in a book, and when the plane was just about fully loaded, I heard a man say, "Is anyone sitting here?"

I looked up at the man. "No," I said.

He sat down in the aisle seat and placed the paper bag he was carrying under his seat. He was Latino, about five foot seven and 150 pounds. He had short black hair cut around his ears and was in his early forties. He was a quiet man who seemed to be troubled by something.

I decided to make small talk. "Are you from Chicago?"

"No, just on my way back home to New York. I was just visiting a friend."

"My name is Robert."

"I'm Edwin," he said, and we shook hands.

I could tell this man had been through something painful. He seemed subdued. Somewhat quietly, he asked, "What about you?"

"Oh, I am going to a conference in New York."

"What kind of conference is it?"

"It's for a community and service organization. Its main focus is on changing a person's attitude by practicing virtuous and common principles."

At this point he perked up a little bit and turned more toward me. "Well, how do you do that?"

I started to answer, but he held up a finger to stop me. He reached under his seat and pulled out the bag. "You're not going to believe this, but I've been searching for something just like what you're describing for over a year now."

He reached into the bag and pulled out a book. It was clear from the title and cover art that this was a book about spirituality. It was not related to my practice; nevertheless, I got goose bumps just seeing it because I knew instantly the reason I was supposed to go to New York.

He began to share his story with me. "I was married for seventeen years, and my wife died last year. I was devastated."

"I'm so sorry," I said. "Did you have kids?"

"No. But, Robert, I was so in love with my wife. We loved each other so much. She was my soul mate, and I miss her terribly. I've been searching for answers and have not been able to find any up to now. It's been hard for me to go on. I wanted to know why she had to die, and I need peace in my life. I don't understand why she died but finally accepted that she did. I haven't been sleeping. I haven't been at peace with myself since this happened, over a year ago. Although I searched and tried many things to help me attain peace and understanding, I have been unable to find it."

His eyes welled up with tears as he spoke about his profound love for his wife. He touched my heart, and tears started welling up in my eyes too. I really had a connection to this man. I felt profound empathy and compassion for him, and I truly felt his pain. This was a powerful experience for me.

He wasn't angry, blaming others or God for his wife's death. He was humbly searching for answers and trying to find some serenity that would let him recapture at least some of the happiness he'd had with his wife. I really wanted to ease this man's suffering.

I shared with him some of what I had learned about how thought shapes our lives. I listened to him pour out his grief. It wasn't a long plane ride, but by the time we got to New York he was calmer and more centered. He thanked me for my words, and we went our separate ways.

I hadn't wanted to go New York because I wasn't listening to the call from my higher self. This was one of those situations in which I didn't want to take the call because I assumed I knew better. My ego had emerged, and because of it I could have missed a wonderful opportunity to change someone's life, to fill it once again with happiness and joy for someone who was virtually at a dead end. Sometimes things are arranged for us, but we don't understand them. We may even try to fight them. If we do, we may lose a wonderful opportunity to learn and grow. As much as our encounter benefitted Edwin and put him on a new path with a different outlook, I felt I benefitted just as much. It helped me open my eyes even more to pay attention to the calls from my higher self and not resist them. I was learning that if I answered the calls, I'd be connected to a higher level. I understood more clearly that if I decided to ignore such a call, I might miss an opportunity for a valuable lesson.

CHAPTER 48

FIRESTORM
SUMMONED FOR
SURRENDER

I t's expensive to bring up a family, and it seemed I was just treading water. We could never seem to get ahead, and when we did something unexpected came up that took all our money. Even though I'd been working in real estate full time since 2002, we were still barely making ends meet. There were periods when we were okay financially for a while, but they didn't last too long. We'd had to sell our townhome, but that money didn't go far. It seemed like we were always concerned about rent, car payments, and just basic necessities. Our focus seemed to be on surviving, not living.

After selling our townhome in Streamwood, we had enough money to pay six months in advance for rent. With the real estate market on an upswing, we were confident we could rent for a couple of years then purchase the home we were renting. It was in a terrific neighborhood with a community pool for the kids. But we felt out of place in this neighborhood because the homes were slightly upscale and a definite upgrade from where we were. We felt like we didn't deserve to be here. At the time, I was still struggling with the old paradigms of my life. They were all about inferiority and not deserving success. They were deeply rooted in the experiences of my younger life, and as they do with many people, they persisted into adulthood.

As years went by, I started working for another real estate company. Going into my third year with the new company, I made more money in the first six months of the year than I'd made in an entire year at any other job I had. Previously, we'd simply been keeping up with our bills, business expenses, and other financial obligations. By no means were we taking vacations or buying luxury items. We were just able to maintain the status quo.

Now it looked like everything was changing, but then came the collapse of the real estate and financial markets. I didn't close another deal the remainder of the year. My business partner offered us money to pay our rent when we needed it and when he could afford to do so. Although we appreciated his kindness, we weren't able to make up any ground. We were bailing water from a sinking ship. We soon failed to pay our rent one month, which became two, and we could not make enough to catch up. I put more pressure on myself, which wasn't helping me. With four kids, I was doing what I could to figure a way out of this mess. On occasion, my wife would have to visit the local food pantry.

I wasn't sure why this was happening to us. The financial hardships kept coming like waves rolling onto the shore, one after the other. No matter how hard I tried we never seemed to be able to get ahead. I felt like I didn't have a chance for my situation to change. The despair and hopelessness my wife and I felt weighed heavy on my heart and mind. Things got very tough. My wife was home watching the children and homeschooling them, and I was working my fingers to the bone but not getting any deals closed. We had no money coming in, and we needed to get on welfare and Medicaid. We also needed food stamps so we could eat.

I thought of quitting and getting another job, but it was too complicated. If I got calls from past clients or new ones who wanted to see properties right away, what could I tell them? There were no buyers of homes to be found, money dried up for loans, and home values dropped precipitously. We fell behind on our payments on our van, and it was eventually repossessed.

This time we fell several months behind on our rent and were not able to catch up. Remarkably, the landlord never gave us a hard time and rarely called us asking for his money. Usually, I'd be the one calling him, telling him we were going to be late again. Fortunately, the man we were renting from was a real estate agent and felt our pain. I didn't see that this was going to get better any time soon, and I didn't want to put him through any further hardship because of us. I knew the man was well-off, but still we were not paying our rent and were at least six months behind. I decided to do one of the hardest things in my life. I went to his office and told him I couldn't pay him any longer. I promised we'd move out, and I thanked him for putting up with us as long as he did.

I could have handled the situation just fine if it had only been me, but it wasn't. It was my wife and our four small children, too. I felt like such a failure. I'd let my family down tremendously. No matter how hard I'd tried, I couldn't seem to escape failure. It had plagued me since I was a young child. I couldn't figure out what was going on. My problems seemed to be getting worse as I got older.

My mom came from poverty. I believe all of those thoughts were programmed into me and became acceptable to me on a subconscious level. They created my poverty paradigm before I was five years old. I had all those thoughts, feelings, and vibrations of not having money, accepting poverty and lack. I felt that was just the way it was. I believed rich people were bad; they didn't earn their money honestly. I didn't want to be like them. I know I picked up all these thoughts when I was little. That's why money and abundance would stay away from me. All those outdated, obsolete sayings, like "Money doesn't grow on trees," were all programs to keep me thinking about lack instead of thinking about abundance. But how was I supposed to know this back then?

I was getting desperate. I sensed we were going to end up homeless. I'd lived on the streets before. I could handle that. But now I was about to drag my wife and kids into it too. Why was all this happening?

A couple of weeks later, a friend who was using my services to sell her home was moving out of state, and her home was going to be vacant very soon. I talked with her and explained our situation, and she allowed us stay there rent free. It was a very small two-bedroom townhome. After coming out of a 2800-square-foot home, this was very difficult. Nonetheless, we were all very grateful for being there and for her kindness.

Still, after being there for a week or so, it started to sink in that we were living as vagrants. I started to reflect more deeply on myself and where I was spiritually and why this was all happening. I felt I was making my wife and children suffer because of my lack of ability or understanding. At times, though, I thought this might actually be good for our kids in some way, even though it pained me for them to live this way. I'm not sure the two youngest ones really knew what was happening. I'm pretty sure the oldest two did. Our youngest two children had a positive attitude. Everything was an adventure.

I reflected deeply about my thought patterns for the last twenty years, especially about money. I thought I had been changing my thought patterns, and I might have been superficially, but then I realized I hadn't been making efforts to correct my subconscious programming and paradigms. I came to believe I was allowed to go through this experience for a reason. Why was I in this position? I kept asking myself that over and over again.

CHAPTER **49**

HEAT OF
THE FIRE

This was the beginning of a deeper, longer look at life as a whole and into my thinking patterns. I began to reflect on my inner self or higher self. I began to open myself up to inspirational and other spiritual influences: movies, books, videos. I watched *The Secret*, and I saw Bob Proctor for the very first time. I began to look into other self-improvement techniques. Proctor in particular seemed to resonate with me, although I didn't start looking at his stuff more deeply until a few years later. The same was true of Dr. Joe Dispenza from *What the Bleep Do We Know?* I began to see that we can actually reprogram our brains and overwrite old paradigms with new, positive ones. I was captivated and had an insatiable appetite to learn as much as I could about this. I looked at anything I could use to try to trigger something inside me so that I could get a firmer grip on what was happening and understand why this had happened to me. I thought maybe it would help to change things for me. Even so, at least for the moment, there was no apparent change in our situation.

I kept trying to generate real estate business. My partner ended up selling his house before he also fell too far behind. He moved into a small rental a third the size of his previous place. In May of 2008, six months after we'd moved into the borrowed townhouse, it was sold and we needed to move again. We had been trying relentlessly to find a home to move into with a land contract and no money, but we had no success. Not too surprising, but at the time I couldn't think of anything else.

Trying to remain positive, but not realizing positivity alone was not going to change my situation, we packed up our belongings and moved more items into storage. We had no place to go and only about a hundred bucks to our name. We couldn't help but think we were going to be living on the street. While my family waited, I went driving around in the van with all that we owned packed to the top. I was trying to find a hotel we could stay at for free.

I drove to a nearby hotel looking for a place to stay for a few days so I'd have time to figure out what we were going to do. I was hoping they would have some pity on me and let us stay a couple of days for free. After my third hotel with the same result, I surrendered to the fact that nobody cared about our situation or us. My negotiating skills were not as good as I thought, and I was obviously not successful.

I called my siblings and my wife called her brother to see if they would help. Much to our surprise, they really didn't have any compassion for our situation at all and wouldn't offer any financial assistance. I never asked for help from anyone, but when I really needed it, we couldn't count on anyone.

Shortsighted and focused only on my family, I was becoming very disgusted with humanity, especially with our family members. How could they not help us? Didn't they realize how dire our circumstances were? I would always try to help people when they were down and out. Instead of looking inside, I became very upset, even angry, with the fact that people didn't want to help us. I felt humiliated and degraded as a man, husband, father, and human being. What kind of man can't support his family? I was extremely hard on myself.

I was in tremendous despair, but I always believed this was happening for a reason. I realize now, in retrospect, it was for my own good. I wouldn't have learned the lessons I did if someone had helped me. I wouldn't have been able to look at my negative thought patterns, my paradigm, and work on changing it. I would have continued to go through life oblivious to the fact that my thoughts created things and I had created my own reality and the mess I was in by the way I'd thought up to that point.

With no other options, I called my mother to see if she would help. She'd always been there to help me in my time of need, and fortunately this time was no different. Being forty-five and having to call my mother because I couldn't support my family was quite humiliating for me. But she didn't make me feel bad. She just offered to help.

She paid for a hotel for a couple of days, which turned into a couple of weeks as we agonized over our next move. We didn't even use the pool while we were there because we were so stressed out and worried about what we were going to do and where we were going to go next. I was trying to be as positive as I could, but I was still mired in negativity. At the time, I understood superficially this was for the better, but my other feelings and emotions seemed to come to the forefront, and gratitude was not among them. Why was our financial situation not changing?

Despite our dire circumstances, we tried to keep as much normalcy in our lives as possible. The kids continued baseball and their other activities, and I did what I could to bring in new business.

CHAPTER **50**

A MIRAGE

I didn't know who my friends were till times got really bad. Some turned out to be fair-weather friends, but when we went all the way down, I could see who was going to stick by us. Two weeks went by, and a couple we knew learned about our situation and offered to open their home to us. They had their downstairs fixed up as an in-law suite. They said we could stay there as long as we liked. We really didn't want to impose, but we had no other choice. We were very grateful for their kind hearts. Their basement was a lot smaller, about a third of the size of the previous place.

The living quarters were very small for six people. There were two bedrooms. I stayed in one with Lynn and our two youngest. The room was about ten by ten. There was barely enough room to walk around the bed. It was cramped, but there were a couple of windows, so we didn't feel too claustrophobic.

My wife, our youngest daughter, and I slept in the bed. Our son slept on the floor beside us. Our two older daughters slept on cots in the other room, which was a bit larger.

There was a small kitchen with a wobbly wooden table. The sink, cabinets, and small fridge were all on one wall.

After being there for several months and still no change in our situation, we felt it was time to move on but had no place to go. My wife said she felt like a refugee because we used to come in a side door, and there would be the six of us confined in the basement. We weren't actually confined, but we felt like we were. Besides, we just didn't want to impose on our friends any longer.

Out of the blue, my wife's friend called her and told her they were being transferred out of state. Their house was going to be demolished, making way for an industrial site. They offered their house to us for $750 a month. It was a large, old Cape Cod with a barn-shaped garage. It stood on an acre of land in a quiet, fifteen-house neighborhood—so $750 would have been a steal in any other circumstances. But I thought at the time that would be a stretch for us. Still, after having the six of us in that three hundred-square-foot, two-room basement, we felt like we were in the lap of luxury. Initially, at least.

It turned out the house had a terrible mold problem. Items that we put in the basement became covered with mold. And there were mice everywhere. They'd scurry along the baseboards and pop their heads out of the stove and the toaster. They chewed up our shoes and clothing. I was just glad they didn't chew on us. We tried to make the best of the situation. I have to say, I was extremely grateful for both the tiny basement and the mouse-infested palace. When you don't have a choice and you don't have money, your standards and expectations in living arrangements change.

The one room in the house that was semi-inviting was the family room, which had pine tongue-and-groove paneling. It felt like a lodge. Well, sort of, but at any rate, the entire family gravitated to that room, and we spent a lot of time there together.

Then I meet someone through a friend who told me about commodities deals we could put together and that there was a huge pot of gold waiting for us at the end of the rainbow. Being desperate, and willing to try anything at this point, I went along with it. I believed I could do it and that it would change our entire situation overnight. In the end, I wasted a year on nothing but a pipe dream. I should have been able to see that, but our circumstances clouded my judgement.

CHAPTER 51

DRAGONFLY

By having no money it felt like I was drowning. I kept sinking. I was looking around for something to grab onto; I didn't find anything that would stop me from going to the bottom. It put a lot of pressure on my marriage and the rest of our family. Things were clamping down on us even tighter financially. Our situation was dire. We were completely broke, had no money coming in, and I was trying to land the big fish. I ended up neglecting my family's well-being and my real estate business.

I was always thinking I was going to close a huge deal, hit the jackpot, instead of working for a living like most people. Although there's a process—a method to manifest things, to change your reality—I just wasn't aware of how to do it and get aligned with it at the time. I only wanted to help my family. How could I develop the right mentality? How could I change my negative thinking? I tried, and nothing seemed to change for any extended period of time. Any gains were always short-lived.

We had to start selling off a lot of our belongings that we could do without: furniture, clothes, CDs, small appliances—anything we could to try and keep gas in the cars and food on the table. We now frequented food pantries regularly and conserved what we did have. We were beyond desperate.

Our gas was shut off, so we had to warm pots of water on the electric stove and pour them into a camping shower bag, then carry them upstairs in order to have warm water to take a shower This went on for a couple of weeks. We really had only the bare essentials left. Our situation seemed hopeless. If it wasn't for my mom, I think I might have given up a long time ago. Finally, we ran out of food. After a short discussion, my wife and I decided to sell the last valuables we owned—our wedding rings.

We knew our love for one another was strong and constant. The rings were only the material aspect, which had no impact on our love.

We couldn't afford to make the payments on the van we'd bought two years earlier, and it was about to be repossessed. Our family was too large to be able to travel legally in one car. We were just going through too much at that moment. Losing our van would cause even more hardship. We just couldn't handle it right then. Knowing it wasn't the right thing to do, this time I was going to refuse to hand over our van like I did the last one. They were going to have to find it and take it from us. We had a pretty good game of hide and seek going with the repo man.

After about five months, the repo man finally found out where we lived, but we never kept the van there. Since my wife was the primary driver of the van, I told her to be very careful to always check and make sure no one was following her before she picked up the van. If she was followed, she was to avoid anywhere we frequented. We didn't want the repo man getting any more of a line on how we lived our lives. He would constantly call us and taunt us, as if we didn't have enough going on in our lives at the time. This just made me even more determined to keep him from getting it.

At this point we were getting ready to move yet again. Due to the market conditions, the deal for the industrial complex on the property where we were living fell apart. Then the owner of the house lost his job in Ohio and wanted to move back, so he wanted us out.

The next time the repo man called, I said, "Okay, you want the van, come by the house tomorrow at eleven a.m. and you can pick it up."

He was happy, thinking he was finally going to accomplish his job. But by the time he got there the next day, we were long gone. We'd moved out the previous day right after I spoke to him. We got a call at 11:05, and we all knew who it was. I would have loved to be there to see his face when he looked in the window and realized we had moved. We were all laughing hysterically and picturing the look on his face. He never saw that coming. In any case, my wife got careless one day about five months later, and he finally got us. At least those extra months really helped us out.

I spent the next month and a half scouring neighborhoods for homes we could move into cheaply. I finally found a house for sale in Elgin. It was in the courts for repossession by the bank. I spoke to the agent, who said it was also a divorce situation. We were able to speak with the owner, the wife, and she agreed to let us have it as a three-month rental before the sheriff's sale, which was the process it had to go through before it went back to the bank.

One day while trying to get some work done in my office, which was in the living room, I heard a key in the door. A man walked in and said, "What are you doing in my house?"

I rose from the table, startled, bewildered. "Your house?"

"I own this house."

"I have a lease," I said. I turned to the file cabinet to retrieve the lease.

"Let me see it," he said, angrily.

I looked over my shoulder, exasperated. "Sure, I'm getting it. It's with your wife. You didn't know about it?"

"No, she didn't tell me. We actually split up. I have all the kids. That should tell you something about her." He looked over the lease and calmed down considerably. "Tell you what," he said, looking up from the paperwork. "You can pay me from now on. I'll do the same lease with you."

I shrugged. "Okay. That's fine with me."

It made no difference to me. The first three-month lease was up, and I had no problem with him. I just needed a place for my family to live. As I suspected, I didn't get my deposit back from the wife.

It was a four-bedroom house in a good neighborhood, and it had originally been very nice. By the time we moved in, it was very beat up. Their fifteen-year-old boy was autistic and had violent fits. There were over fifty places where the drywall was either punched in or smashed in. A couple of the kitchen cabinet doors had been painted red, and several of the cabinets had been broken along with all the upstairs doors and doorframes. There were floor tiles missing or cracked. There was a bunch of junk the owners had left behind in the garage and basement that I needed to get rid of. The garage door was broken and had to be manually opened and closed. It was a wreck. But it kept the rain and snow off our heads, and it was warm inside.

In 2010 I started losing faith in my partner's ability to grow his company as he'd said he would. Nothing had changed, and based on what I understood of his business model, I was definitely not being paid properly. The way it was set up, I would have to sell fives houses to equal the commission on one sale by any other agent. The volume of business he envisioned was not developing. Opportunities to get us back on our feet were passing me by. After more than a year contemplating, I decided to move on and start my own company.

One evening at eleven, at the end of September of 2010, I became frustrated with trying to think of a name for my new company. I thought I should finally just quit real estate altogether and do something else. I was disgusted with everything, and I decided to go to bed. As I turned off the light and headed upstairs, I heard a fluttering sound in the living room, which was my office. I stopped and listened and heard nothing. When I headed back up the stairs, I heard it again.

I went back into the living room and flipped on the lights. I looked around and didn't see anything immediately, then my eyes caught the picture above the fireplace. It was a picture of me and my wife back in 1989, in front of a shrine with a massive gold roof. Next to the picture was a huge dragonfly about eight inches long. How did that get in here? I wondered. It was light blue with black marbled lines through it. It was right next to the picture. A dragonfly in our house at the end of September? How can this be? I thought.

I looked at the dragonfly, then looked at the picture. I looked from one to the other again and again. And then I noticed that the dragonfly was next to the golden roof on the shrine. I thought to myself, golden roof—Golden Roof Realty. That's it!

I'd been so frustrated by my lack of ability to think of a name, and there it was. This wasn't something I thought of. It was given to me. It was one of those calls from my higher self that I'd had such a hard time hearing and answering in the past. If this had happened a few years earlier, maybe I would have just grabbed the dragonfly, put it outside, and never thought anything more of it. But now I realized I was getting better at hearing the call and answering it. It seemed like I was finally getting in tune with what I needed to change in my life and to be open to the help I needed in order to do that.

I shut off the light and turned to go upstairs. I decided I wanted to get one more look at the dragonfly and to set it free. After all, it had just assisted me in naming my new company. I turned the light back on, and the dragonfly was gone! I didn't hear any fluttering. I looked all around the living and dining rooms and even in the kitchen. It was nowhere to be found. It was like it had simply vanished.

CHAPTER 52

FACING TIMELESS TRUTH

I was slowly trying to dig out of my financial hole. Business was still slow for me, but I was able to get a few listings here and there. One of the listings was one of the more expensive homes I'd had in recent years. It was a divorce situation, and the man was a drunk. Due to his drinking, he had lost his million dollar business, alienated his wife and kids, received numerous DUIs, had his car repossessed, been arrested a couple of times, and had been in and out of the hospital numerous times after falling down or going in to sober up. He was the poster child for how alcohol can ruin your life. He had a beautiful wife and kids, but he apparently loved vodka more than he did them.

After more than a year, his home eventually sold. It closed in September 2011, which netted me the highest commission I had ever made. It seemed I rarely if ever got "the big deal." Although I was grateful for the smaller ones, things would be a heck of a lot easier if I got four or five of these types of listings closed every year. That was the majority of my income that year. As my negative thinking habits would come to the fore, that money would soon be spent in a way that it wasn't intended for.

August 2011, just after my fiftieth birthday, things seemed to be going well. My relationship with my wife, Lynn, had never been better. Our love seemed to be so deep for one another. As strange as it sounds, after being married twenty-five years, I truly felt the best I ever had about my wife. Lynn and I had never been closer. At least with all the challenges we faced—financial, no permanent home, etc.—we still had each other. She would always be there for me.

We decided to go up to Wisconsin Dells for the weekend for some well overdue family time. We had to take two cars, as we usually did if we went anywhere as a whole family. The two youngest had been almost too young to enjoy much the last time we'd been to the Dells. Now they could enjoy all the water slides and have some thrills instead of panic attacks. After the first day of fun, we had dinner with the kids, and then Lynn and I decided to get back out for more cocktails. It was getting late, and we were chatting idly, and she mentioned something about her second boyfriend.

I sat up straighter, a puzzled look on my face. "What did you say? Did you just say your second boyfriend? You never told me you had a second boyfriend. Before we were married, you told me you'd only had one boyfriend, and he left you for someone else."

She blushed deeply and stammered a bit. Then she held up her glass. "This is my third. I don't know what I said."

"Well, I know what you said. How many other guys did you date?"

"Why does that matter?" she said. "It was over twenty-five years ago."

"Because when we were going out, before we got married, I remember I specifically asked you and you told me you had only one, now you are saying there were two? Or, how many? How many more were there?"

"I don't know. You expect me to remember?"

"Yes," I said.

By this time I was feeling very uneasy, uncomfortable about what I was told. I was breaking out in a cold sweat and could not believe what she had just let slip out. Did it matter how many guys she'd dated? Not at all. But it mattered that she'd deceived me. Because of what happened with my mom, I despise lying. She lied to me.

"So tell me, how many guys were you with before we got married?"

"Why do want to know that?"

"I told you, before we got married you said you were with only one guy and had only one boyfriend. But there was more than one, right?"

"Yes, okay, but they weren't all my boyfriends, some were just dates."

"What the hell?" I said, leaning back in my chair, stunned. "You lied to me."

I felt totally duped, manipulated. She'd violated my trust, and now it came out after all these years. I couldn't care less if it was two or two hundred. The problem I had was that she'd lied to me. She'd deliberately deceived me. Just when we were at the pinnacle of our relationship, just when I thought no matter what else happened in my life, I'd have my wife who was always honest and trustworthy, always there for me. It took the life out of me. I felt a deep sense of betrayal.

"How could you lie to me?"

"Robert, it was over twenty-five years ago. It's in the past."

"Yeah, I know, but why did you have to lie about it?"

"Well, if I told you, you might not have married me."

"What? That should be my decision, not yours. So you manipulated me into marrying you?"

I had always protected myself from manipulation and was always careful about people getting close to me until I knew I could trust them. This just ruined the rest of the weekend. I was speechless. And she just seemed to have a smug look on her face like she got away with it. I didn't want to talk to her anymore, and I couldn't wait to get the hell out of there and go home. If it wasn't for the kids I would have left. I got up from the table and went for a long walk that night.

After we got to our home the next day, my wife decided to go out for a while with the two youngest. After she left, I called her and asked for her Facebook password.

"What do you want that for?" she said.

"I just want to check on something."

"Sure," she said, and she gave it right over to me.

Looking around her page, I noticed she was friends with some men I didn't know. I went into her messages, and much to my surprise I found some correspondence between her and a few guys, and with one she had quite a few messages. They seemed flirtatious, but there was nothing overt in them. Still, my stomach dropped and my heart started to pump faster and harder. I felt sick. I couldn't believe what I'd just read. I decided to print some of this stuff out to read later.

The next day we went out and had a few drinks and dinner. When I got to my second cocktail, I leaned across the table and spoke in a low voice. "Lynn, I want to know if there's anything else you want to tell me. I just want you to be honest with me. I don't care if you slept with someone or went out with someone. You have amnesty. I just want the entire truth. I'm not going to get mad or upset."

She shook her head and smiled gently. "There is nothing else. This was the only time I communicated with him."

"Are you sure? I implore you, if there is something you need to tell me, please tell me now."

"Rob," she said, exasperated.

I held up a hand. "Wait. To show you how much I want you to be honest with me, I want to open my heart and be honest with you about something."

"Okay," she said, somewhat subdued.

"I never told you this before, or anyone for that matter, because I was embarrassed, and it hurt me tremendously as a child. This contributes to my trust issues, so I want you to know just how important it is for me to have you be honest with me."

I went on to tell her that I was a runaway and that I'd been sexually abused. After I finished my story, I continued to plead with her. "So honesty and trust are very important to me. Are you sure there's nothing else?"

She reached across the table and put her hand on mine. "No, there's nothing else to tell you."

I knew I would have to try to overcome these feelings of betrayal at having been lied to before we were married. I knew it was a long time ago, but I really felt like I was taken advantage of and manipulated into marrying her. The next day, trying to figure out how I was going to overcome this challenge, I decided to review our phone bills for the last year or so to confirm what she was telling me was true. I couldn't believe what I found. There had been phone calls and texts between her and the guy she was after in high school. I was totally and completely devastated. I felt the life force had gone out of my body. I'd given her every opportunity to be honest with me, to come clean and tell me everything. I went back to read over some of the old messages I'd printed out to see if I could make more sense out of them. It was all coming into focus now.

Late that night, I confronted her once again. I tried to stay calm, but I felt so insecure, and my blood began to boil. For the very first time in twenty-five years, my emotions got the best of me. I started yelling at her at the top of my lungs. What I felt was fragility, but it came across as anger. I was completely vulnerable and I had to cover it with something so it didn't show. Anger was a handy disguise that I had a lot of experience with.

"You fucking lied to me. Again! I poured my heart out to you yesterday, and you still lied to me. How could you do that to me?"

"You would have gotten upset."

"I told you yesterday even if you slept with the guy, I would not have liked it, but I would have appreciated your honesty and worked through it. But now that you had that chance and continued to lie, what did you expect? Of course I am going to be upset!"

"Rob, I didn't sleep with him," she said. "I never even met with him. The only contact I had with him was on Facebook and the occasional text and phone call."

Our plan was to try to do this in private, but our voices had gotten out of control, and by this time all the kids heard us arguing. They knocked on the bedroom door and we had to calm them down. They were all upset. Before that night, in all our twenty-five years of marriage, we'd argued maybe once before. And it wasn't like that night. That's what made it all the worse for everyone.

I just couldn't stay in the house with her any longer. My younger kids cried, and I told them it wasn't their fault, that mom and dad were just having a little problem they needed to overcome. That was partly an act for their sake. I was so wound up that I needed to get out here. I felt like this argument was the one thing that could legitimately destroy our marriage.

I drove around for a while and decided to check into a hotel a few towns away. My life had just been turned upside down. What was amazing to me was that just over a month ago I'd remarked about how my wife was always standing by me through the tough times, and we were getting along better than any other time in our marriage. Now look where we were! At that moment, I didn't care if I ever saw my wife again.

What I'd learned in the last few days was something I thought I'd never have to address with her. As they say, love is blind. I was mad at myself for being so stupid, gullible, and unaware of what was happening. Interestingly, six months before this incident, I'd asked her if there was anything going on in her life she wasn't telling me about. I simply asked her innocently, in a nonjudgmental way. I had no reason to suspect anything. I just threw it out there and absolutely didn't expect anything. I'd asked her because it seemed like no matter how hard I tried at work, I wasn't able to put any deals together. I thought maybe something was out of sync with us.

Of course, I overreacted. Lynn was human, and we'd had a great marriage for twenty-five years. Should I have just forgiven her without question? If I'd been a little more aware of my higher self, it would have been a lot easier. But I hadn't learned as much as I needed to. I was flawed, too, and I let my past get the best of me for a time.

But my marriage still meant something to me, even though I had to wonder if it would last much longer. My kids were very upset that I was gone and didn't want to come home. Whether they knew it or not, they were much better off this way. Still, it was hard for me to be away from my kids.

After all the things I'd been through in my life, you'd think this would not bother me so much. But for some reason, it really hit me hard, more than anything else. Now, in retrospect, I see that this all tied back to my mom. When she tried to end my life ... that was the ultimate betrayal. So any sense of betrayal from a woman who was supposed to have my back was almost more than I could take.

My issues were very deep-seated. Over the course of our marriage, there were times when Lynn and I had minor disagreements, and as I sat down at the dinner table to eat something she'd prepared, just for a split second, I wondered if she might have poisoned it. Of course that had nothing to do with Lynn and everything to do with my trust issues— the crushing baggage I'd carried with me all my life due to my mother's attempt to murder me.

But now all that came back to me with such force. It was like someone had swept my legs out from under me, but instead of hitting the ground face first, I felt I kept falling, like I was falling into a deep hole, and if I ever did hit bottom, I'd be so deep there'd be no way to climb out of it ever again. I looked up at the ceiling of my hotel room like I was looking up out of that hole. "I quit," I said out loud. "I can't take it anymore, God! You win. I know I'm a huge loser, but how much can one person take anyway?"

I just didn't care anymore. I really only wanted to leave this world. I'd had enough. I gave up. After everything I'd been through in my life, I was finally broken as a man. I could not overcome life's challenges anymore. My will to carry on melted away like the snow around a fire.

That was how I felt, even though at that point in my life I had a deeper understanding of why things had happened. I started to think that if everything happened for a reason, then this was happening for a reason too. But at the time, I couldn't make the connection between the spiritual, the mental, and the physical, so my suffering continued. My wife was the only thing I was clinging to. Now she, too, had been stripped away from me.

On several occasions a mutual friend counseled my wife and I together and encouraged me to move back home and to work through this situation. After the last time we talked, I decided to go back home. I went home after nearly a month of being away from my kids.

CHAPTER 53

WHAT LED ME WAS LOVE

I t's hard to earn back trust, and I had been through so many disappointments in my life that it was doubly hard for me. Although I made the decision to move forward, without a doubt it was one of the most challenging things I had to do in my life. Although I was home, I still felt apart from Lynn.

Back at home, even though I tried, it was very hard for me not to be judgmental. The littlest things would set me off and bring up the topic again. I don't know how many times we revisited the issue. I had a difficult time forgiving and letting go back then. It was easier for me to just walk away, remove myself from the problem. That was my version of problem solving. Just put it in a box in the back of my mind's closet. But this was too complicated to handle that way. It wasn't just me I had to think about. I had kids now. And I didn't feel like I had a partner to help me with the problem. The one person I'd always relied for the past twenty-five years seemed to be a distant memory.

I tried to put on a facade in front of my kids, to act like everything was okay. I was cordial with my wife, but the effort of it made me feel like I was carrying a hundred-pound box up an endless flight of stairs with a casual smile on my face, pretending it wasn't heavy. I was very morose. I was unhappy at Lynn for deceiving me before we got married. Unhappy that she'd lied to me after we got married. Unhappy she lied to me again, after I bared my soul. Unhappy she was after another man instead of me, especially after how often she'd told me she loved me. Of course, she told me she wasn't after another man. How was I supposed to make sense of that? She wasn't "after" him, she was just "interested" in him? I wasn't sure what the difference was. Could she have been that unhappy with me? Why didn't she ever talk to me about these issues?

I told my wife to go seek counseling so she could figure out why she'd done this, and to her credit she went. After she went a few times she suggested we both go. That was probably her therapist's idea.

I didn't feel like I was the one that should be going, but I realized that if I wanted to save my marriage I would have to do my part too. And it might help. I went for my orientation. I told the intake person that I didn't want to talk to anyone who has had an easy life. I wanted someone who'd had difficult times in their life. I didn't need some pompous ass who'd lived a comfortable life trying to give me advice. I didn't think they'd be able to relate to all I'd been through. I figured for them it was about what they'd gotten from textbooks, and my life didn't fit in a textbook. I knew all too well that experience is the best teacher in life.

The counseling center assigned me to a lady who was divorced. The intake person said, "I know her, and this would be the perfect person for you." I took her word for it and agreed to meet with her.

Lynn and I both had our counselors present during our joint meetings. After a few of these joint sessions, my therapist felt a lot of the anger I had pent up was a byproduct of all the hurt I'd endured in my life. She asked to meet me one-on-one to talk about the issues. In our first of those sessions, I decided not to waste any time or beat around the bush with her. Starting with my childhood, I just laid my life history on the table in a brief but painful one-hour summary.

Weeks, then months, followed and nothing changed much in the relationship between Lynn and me. I seriously wondered if she thought it was a mistake to have gone behind my back or just to have gotten caught at it. Even though she said it was innocent in the beginning, it didn't end up that way. Her actions filled me with doubt about her true feelings toward me.

Something had to give. We were hard pressed to continue our relationship in this manner. The kids were feeling the effects of the rift between their parents. I was not happy. My wife was not happy. And with a dirty stream of emotion trickling down to our kids, they were not happy either. What was I supposed to do? I had to decide if I really wanted a marriage or not. Because I was callused by the events in my life, I thought long and hard about ending my marriage.

In another session, my therapist said, "You have twenty-five years of marriage. Are you going to throw it away for one incident? Does that really outweigh the twenty-five years of all the other good times? Is it worth it?"

Back then my thinking was really screwed up. I had made some progress in the way I saw how I fit into the world around me, but not enough. This episode was a test and a learning experience. I could handle it much better if it happened today. Back then, my wrong-headedness almost destroyed me.

I scooted forward to the edge of the couch. "For me, trust and loyalty is everything. Yes, it would be worth it. My way of thinking about things is different than most people. What I went through in my life hardened my feelings and emotions. The wall around me got thicker and taller with every incident. I'd rather be alone than have to stay with someone who betrayed me and whom I can't trust any longer. I wish I could let it roll off my back like the water in a shower."

Did I really want to subject my kids to the same kind of life I'd gone through? If I got divorced, what would happen to my kids? How would their childhoods go from that point? When they got married and had problems, would they choose to leave as well?

I did think about my kids, but most of my energy was focused on myself, and it was very negative. I was having a big pity party for myself. I just kept asking why I had to go through so much suffering.

I'd been at death's door more than a half dozen times—almost not making it through surgery when I was five, three major car accidents, two motorcycle accidents, being the victim of a premeditated attempted murder (the murder of my self-worth was much more devastating). On top of that, being a runaway, being sexual abused, the homelessness, and so many other hardships weighed on me.

I was able to survive those and continue to lead a productive life. They formed the heavy baggage of my life, but up till now those thoughts had also kept me going, always made me believe my life had some special meaning. Even these thoughts didn't mean much to me any longer. I was made to endure and overcome these challenges for a reason.

I would still reflect on the night that I came out of the bar and saw Carol waiting by the car with her head down. I knew she had volunteered to do something for me, to give me the greatest gift another human could give—life. I didn't want to believe it was a soul contract or a debt she owed. Instead I always believed she was giving me the opportunity to do something with my life that only I was capable of doing. Or maybe it was so I could do something with my life that she was unable to do with hers. She had so much more love for me than I ever knew or would be able to comprehend. Thinking these thoughts would help me get through some of the tough times in my life, and that helped me cope with her passing. If she had a purpose that night, then her death had meaning. And that meant that *my* life had purpose too. I wanted to keep seeking a purpose, a mission that was ordained by this mystical experience that had happened in my life. Apparently, I'm a very slow learner, and I had to fight my way through all the things that seemed to come very naturally to me—the doubting, judging, not paying attention to the call from my higher self, and not believing in me.

CHAPTER **54**

GIVING BIRTH TO A NEW PERSPECTIVE

I was determined to make sure my kids would have easier lives than I did and that they wouldn't have to endure what I did in my childhood. Everybody has an image of how their lives should be. A happy home with a nice house, kids in a good school, and a supportive wife was my image. I didn't really think it could fall apart in an instant, but it can. I knew if this was going to work, I had to face up to the situation and work on trust and bridge building.

Back during that very first therapy session, after I'd told the abbreviated version of my life story to my therapist, I asked her, "In all the time you've been doing counseling, have you ever heard of anyone with a past like mine?"

She didn't even take time to think. "Robert, in my twenty-five-plus years of counseling, I've worked with dysfunctional families, people in abusive relationships, addicts, gang members, and people that were in prison, but I've never heard of anyone going through as much as you have in your life. Typically, someone has one major traumatic event in their life.

For most people, that one event is difficult enough for them to deal with. In some cases, it can become debilitating or destructive for them. After what you've been through, to be where you are now is an accomplishment. For you to be where you are today is remarkable. You're a very strong person."

By everything she just told me, I felt special. That was an important message to me and I am not the only one out there with such experiences.

Dear Reader,

You might have had a
dysfunctional family.

You might have had a difficult childhood.

You might be an addict or
you have been an addict.

You might have been physically,
emotionally, or sexually abused.

You might have been through any number of things in life.

No one will ever look inside you and know
what you experienced, how you felt,
or how you still may feel about it.

There's no contest to see who can carry the most.

You're carrying a lot. You are special and
worthy of having the life you wish for.

You're strong—maybe stronger than you know right now.

Don't give up! Don't you ever give up!

The world needs you.

"I know it's not my doing," I said. "I've always known there's been some higher force that's protected me and pushed me to keep moving forward. Even so, before all this happened with my wife, I didn't feel like I'd done enough and wasn't happy. I should have done more, become more." I thought of all the things I'd started and never followed through on. At that moment, I was on the verge of tears. I felt like I'd wasted my life in a lot of respects. But at the same time, I knew that so much had happened in my life. I'd had so many dramatic experiences. I wiped the tears from my cheeks with both hands and chuckled. "I should write a book," I said in a whisper, almost to myself.

"What was that?" said Carla.

I waved her question away. "Nothing."

"No, Rob, you said something."

"I was just thinking about how crazy my life has been. I said I should write a book."

"What would the book be about?"

I waved my hand between us. "This. Everything I've been telling you."

"Interesting. Who would you be writing to?"

"I don't know," I said. "Just a book."

"Yeah, but who would you want to read it?"

That question caught me off guard. I'd thought about writing a book, but not about who would read it. "I guess … just … people who've been through tough times in their lives. People who've had to struggle. People who've had doubts about who they are. Why they were put here in this life. People like me."

When I looked at her, I saw that she wasn't laughing. This wasn't a joke to her. I got a little rush. Was that possible? That I could write a book that might help other people? I'd felt I wanted to help people. I'd tried to do that trek, but that didn't work out. Maybe this was it. Maybe I could still help people.

"If I could actually write something that people would read, I would hope that it would ease their suffering, give them faith and courage to overcome the difficult times in their lives. They might be inspired and believe that if this guy can go through all this and make it, they can certainly make it through whatever they're going through."

Carla smiled and nodded. "I actually think that's a great idea. I think it would do you a lot of good, and I think it might very well give other people hope and inspire them to keep moving forward in their lives."

I felt like I'd been dead, and then someone hit me with a defibrillator to bring me back to life. I was still lying on the table in the ER, but I was breathing again. I was alive. The jolt had saved me.

I always enjoyed helping people and I always seemed to have the ability to become passionate when I talked. Since I have a wealth of experience in overcoming adversity, when I shared words of encouragement about difficult times others are facing, sometimes I would talk so passionately that I would move them to tears. I believe I was really getting through to them. It surprised me that I was able to get so passionate about what I was talking about. It touched me, too.

Years ago, when my older sister got married, she asked me to say a few words at the church, and they wrote something and gave it to me. I just folded it and put it in my pocket.

"Aren't you going to read it?" my sister said.

"No," I said. "I'll read it at the church."

I took a quick look at it when we arrived at the church. When I got up to the podium, before I started reading, I was very relaxed. I gave a great speech. More than likely it had a lot to do with being young and cocky.

Recently, my apparent ability to communicate began to motivate me to see if I could help others by talking with them when the opportunity arose. If I could move them in an honest, caring, and loving manner, this was a sign for me that what I was saying was getting through to them, and just maybe it would give them some direction that would help change their lives. That fills me with joy, knowing that I can have a positive effect on someone's life.

That is what motivates me above all else.

The therapy truly made a difference in my marriage. But also, I think the decision to write the book helped a lot. For me to have a direction and hope that I could do something positive helped to change my outlook. I realized that I'd let my past negativity and distrust color my view of Lynn and her actions. I saw that she loved me as much as I loved her. She hadn't done anything I couldn't forgive her for.

As strange as it might seem to some, I came to know that my mother's actions weren't beyond forgiveness either. For years, I couldn't make sense of what she'd tried to do to my sisters and me. Eventually, I decided to make an effort to understand her feelings. It was difficult, and I still may not understand completely, but I'm guessing it might have been part of the plan for my life. Certainly, if it hadn't happened, I wouldn't be who I am today. And even though what happened was unimaginable, unthinkable, today I know my mother's mental breakdown was a kind of emotional thunderstorm and that getting through that storm eventually led her to a better place in her life. What my mother did to my sisters and me changed our destiny and hers. Today I know she loves us, and I've forgiven her completely.

CHAPTER 55

THE LAST CALL FOR DOUBT AND THE NEW BEGINNING

To me, writing a book was a huge undertaking. People don't just go off and write about their mothers trying to kill them when they were children and all the problems that creates throughout their lives. For some reason I knew this will be a huge step. But after I left therapy that afternoon, I went home and began giving serious consideration to writing a book. Like most of the things in my life up to this point, I started doubting myself and finding all the reasons not to do it instead of the reasons to do it.

But this time, before totally ruling out the possibility of success, just to make certain I wasn't making another mistake in my life or selling myself short again, I prayed and asked for a sign. I didn't go within because I simply didn't understand the process or importance of doing that yet. So, sitting on the couch and looking out the window, I was staring at a huge oak tree across the street. "Please help me," I said. "Is this what I'm supposed to do? If it's my mission to write this book to try and help others, let me know in no uncertain terms. Please let me have a sign. Have a tree branch fall across the street."

Staring at that big old oak tree, I noticed that a branch toward the top was hanging down. I told myself that didn't count. That could have been there a while. I kept looking and nothing. I went upstairs not expecting anything and was somewhat relieved because I thought I wouldn't be able to write a book anyway. I woke up the next day thinking I was still crazy and not knowing how I would write a book.

I went downstairs for coffee and stopped at the front window to look outside and check the weather. It was a clear, sunny day, and I smiled at the prospect of getting out into it. But as I started to turn away from the window, I did a double take. I was floored by what I saw. This monster tree limb—not a branch, but a limb—had fallen! It looked like it was at least two feet in diameter and twelve feet long. I guess somebody wanted to get their point across. There was no mistaking that message. It was like the gas starter on a fireplace. Suddenly the flame ignited in my belly. It seemed to burn away the shell I was in, and I began to come alive again. The thought of writing a book was the inspiration that gave my life purpose.

This blew me away, I couldn't believe how deliberate and lucid this message was. I didn't care—I needed to find a way to get it done. I was definitely inspired to write the book, and I knew it was what I had to do. Even so, I still had doubts.

When I managed to put the negative thoughts aside and allow the positive thoughts to come in, I realized that if I were to tell my story, maybe other people would feel better about their own circumstances and would be encouraged to make it through the difficult times in their own lives. The potential far-reaching effect on those who were really searching for something and needed encouragement could be dramatic. These thoughts provided fuel so that the spark inside of me once again ignited the wick of my imagination.

But something was still blocking me from accepting the sign completely. I got the message, but as the days went by, the old doubts returned.

I wondered if I'd just been fooling myself about the sign of the tree limb and fooling myself about writing the book. That began to feel like just one more thing that would fall through the cracks in my life—one more thing I intended to do but never followed through with.

A few weeks later I had a great therapy session. We talked about all the things I hadn't followed through with. I became choked up just thinking about it, and with tears in my eyes, I said, "Like the book, too. I should have kept writing." It was painful. I felt like I understood some things, but I had let my doubts get the best of me and stop my progress once again.

After the session, I left the building, and when I got close to my car, I could not believe what I was looking at! I ran back inside and told the receptionist I had to see Carla again. She came to the door and I asked her to come outside with me. I almost grabbed her by the arm, but I managed to keep myself together. I was leading the way, but I kept turning back and waving her along. "You have to come outside," I said. "I have to show you something. You are not going to believe it!"

Bewildered, she followed me to the parking lot.

When we got out to my car, I said, "Can you believe this? This is what we were just talking about." It was a large tree branch lying right next to my car.

Carla just stood there and stared at the branch for a moment. Then she looked at me with a big smile on her face. "Oh, my gosh. That's amazing."

It was a bright sunny day with no wind that could have dislodged the branch from the tree, and I saw no breaks on any of the trees nearby. There was no mistaking that sign. It was perfectly clear and abolished any remaining doubt in me. I took a picture of it and made it the wallpaper on my phone to remind me to keep writing. This is one of the most positive, life changing, moving experiences I have ever had in my life.

It was a humbling push from below, pushing me upward. I'd gone through so much in my life that hit me over the head in a negative way, so when I was hit over the head with the original sign I received, it didn't have the desired effect. But this sign seemed to be encouraging me with love, and it persuaded me beyond any shadow of a doubt and moved me past the limits I'd always put on myself.

I went home and told my wife. I just started weeping uncontrollably; I was so moved, right down to the heart of my soul. I continued to weep the rest of the night and the next night as well. Just thinking about this, even now, makes the tears well up and chokes me up with emotion. I finally know what I am supposed to be doing with my life. For the first time, my path, my direction in life has become crystal clear.

I need to tell my story, share my experiences with others. I'm hopeful it will give them some inspiration and tenacity to make it through challenging times in their lives. More importantly, I hope it gives them the formula for how to do it. I guess that would be my next book. For once in my life, I was going to see this through in spite of how difficult it was going to be for me or my lack of belief in myself or my lack of skills. I was determined to finish my book.

The idea of harnessing my thoughts and directing them toward what I wanted didn't fully awaken in me for a few years to come. In any case it wasn't easy, and it wasn't fast. I wanted to quit a bunch of times and got sidetracked just as many. When that happened, I began doubting myself again, and I even doubted the message I received, so I had stopped writing for quite some time.

I would realize a few years later that this was due to my paradigm, which caused an inability to make decisions. It was part of the way I'd thought my entire life in a negative, unproductive, self-destructive manner. That old inner-voice was telling me, "You can't do that. You're not a writer. What are you, crazy? You're a high school dropout. You can't even put a grammatically correct sentence together. How the hell are you going to write a book? Everyone has problems, so who wants to hear about someone else's? What good is that going to do for anyone?"

All these thoughts were suffocating my ambitions and limiting my potential to grow or to do something outside of my comfort zone.

Phoenix Rising

Have you heard the saying, God provides in mysterious ways? Now I understand. For me it was only mysterious because I didn't understand how powerful my thoughts were or the process of creation. The stay in our temporary home ended up turning into a year, then two years, then finally the home was headed for foreclosure and the sheriff's sale. This was the longest we'd stayed in one place—almost three years. The real estate market was starting to pick up, and our income was improving slightly, although we still had a difficult time making rent consistently. Regardless, I'd finally had enough of temporary housing and was determined to have a permanent home for my family.

I was learning a little more about how to think properly, but I still didn't fully understand what I was doing or how things were happening, although the picture slowly began to come into focus. I came to understand one principle clearly—when I made a firm decision about what I wanted, this was a key contributor to making it manifest.

In late summer 2012, I found out that my stepmother had passed away after a long bout with health problems. My stepsister said she had many medical bills and that there would be little money, if any, left over. She said we might get a little something after it cleared probate. Although it would have been nice, we really didn't want to count on anything, since she had so many bills to pay.

We still had no place to go after the sale of the house we were in and not enough money to come up with to rent another property. I put a lot of energy into thinking there had to be a way to resolve our problem, and working with the bank and the court, we were miraculously allowed to stay there an additional eight months rent-free, which gave us time to begin seriously looking for and trying to manifest a new home for us. Only this time my thoughts were that we'd find a permanent home. We had no idea how this was going to happen. Still, I made a decision to have a permanent home for our family, and I began to imagine that it would be so.

Due to our credit, we couldn't get a loan, so we wouldn't be able to buy any home. The only chance we had would be if a seller would offer financing. We made offers on over thirty properties but had no success. I stayed positive and kept focusing on us having a permanent home. Eventually, we learned that there actually was a little money coming to us from my stepmother's estate, and we would use it to pay a year of rent somewhere or as a down payment on a house if we could find someone to work with us.

During this time, one of my clients had called to tell me she had to evict her tenants and would need to sell her home. She suggested my wife and I buy it. This was tempting because it was a very nice, newer home in a great neighborhood. But we didn't know if we'd be able to buy it, and my wife and I both agreed that it was too far away from everything we needed to be near.

Not long after, we finally found a place to rent. We agreed with the agent that we'd pay eleven month's rent up front and get one month free. All we had to do was sign the papers in a few days. That was a relief—until the phone rang the day we were supposed to sign. The agent told us that, for whatever reason, the seller had taken the deal off the table. Bummer! Now we were back at square one, and we had to be out of our place in less than thirty days. I asked my wife again about the house my clients wanted to sell to us. We asked our children if they wanted to rent a house or have a more permanent one. Despite the distance, everyone voted without hesitation for a permanent home. The thought of us not having to move again made them all extremely happy. Me too.

We took the children to see the house. Since they, too, had been through so much, I wanted them to take part in the decision. They were all very excited. It was a big change from where we'd been living. It was a gorgeous, spacious house with four bedrooms, two and a half baths, a huge kitchen, a fireplace, a three-car garage, and a full, unfinished basement. The topper, as far as the kids were concerned, was the pool in the backyard. Even with the pool, there was still plenty of room for the garden we dreamed of. I felt they really deserved this after all they had been through.

We decided to talk to my clients to see if they wanted to sell us their house on a land contract. We went out to dinner with them and explained what we'd been through. We told them that, despite our circumstances, we hoped that they would still want to sell us their home.

They were interested. They spoke with their attorney, who advised them against it, but for some reason they still felt compelled to do it. They were going to sleep on it and get back to us. My wife and I were waiting anxiously awaiting their call.

The phone rang and the owner said they would agree, but much to my surprise he said, "I am going to sell you the house outright and do the financing myself."

I was in shock. I thanked him repeatedly and told him how grateful we were for their decision. I almost broke into tears on the phone I was so happy. My wife was ecstatic. The location of the house still made us hesitate; it wasn't ideal for us. But it was such a great deal. We spent days trying to come up with reasons why we should not move there, and each time they called us with an even better arrangement financially. After we hesitated one more time, he called me back and told me they'd decided to lower the already agreed upon interest rate, too. I couldn't believe it! The terms kept getting better and better. The permanent home we'd been yearning for and imagining came into reality after twenty years of negative financial thinking and constant moves.

Now it's been two and a half years since we bought this house. We've made all our payments on time, and we plan to continue doing the same. Because of how slow I was at recognizing my negative thinking patterns, my paradigms, this suffering from financial and housing problems went on for a very long time. It was brutal. I wouldn't wish it on anyone. Throughout this learning experience, despite our dire circumstances, even though this was exceedingly intense and very long and I wanted to take refuge in a hole many times, I was able to weather the storm. Looking back, I realize that my decision to find a permanent home for my family was made with such a firm intention that it was the trigger of the manifestation process that created this reality. Trying to get to the ability to think properly was like trying to bake a cake without knowing what ingredients to use. Somehow you figure it out. I know now, and that's what's most important.

I also created a lot of unnecessary suffering as well by not controlling my thoughts and by letting them run unchecked. I finally figured out why I had to suffer so much, not only during these financial hard times but throughout my life. We attract to ourselves what we think about, more so if those thoughts are energized emotionally. I was in a perpetual downward spiral that was out of control. You can't create or have prosperity when you're thinking or feeling that you're lacking or impoverished. By reading and researching and merging different ideas, I finally figured out what I was doing and what I needed to do to change my circumstances even more. They need to teach this stuff in school. Now I use this process daily to create the life I want. My suffering ended when I became awakened to the divinity within and started managing my thoughts. I understood that we are co-creators. Our thoughts determine what kind of reality we attract to ourselves. Everything that has ever been created in this world started with a thought.

It hadn't seemed so at the time, but my previous hardships were actually blessings. Being homeless stopped me in my tracks and forced me to finally start to reflect on my way of thinking, which was corrupt and perverted. Since I wasn't paying attention to the calls from my higher self, I needed to have an intense emotional and physical crisis to awaken me. I'd been looking at life and at myself wrong all along. In my youth, in my own mind, I was just a weed. But sometimes something springs up that looks like a weed but that later blossoms into a beautiful flower.

Like myself, most people don't change until there's a crisis. Unfortunately, that's what it sometimes takes to get our attention and awaken us to whatever it is we need to awaken to so that we can gain the experience we need for this journey of life.

"Follow your heart" is more than a saying; it's a way of life. But if you're going to follow your heart, you have to make sure your mind and heart are united, harmonized. Actively holding a feeling in your heart is coherence. It's being in the now, the moment. This is the origin of our intuition, our sixth sense, if you will. When you learn to practice coherence, you'll become more in the now, more peaceful, and more in harmony with your higher self—intuition.

Not being coherent and not following my heart caused me so much unnecessary suffering and unhappiness. Now my life flows so much easier because I've learned to listen to my heart.

In order for us to reach our full potential in life, to discover who we truly are, what we're capable of, we must be true and follow our passion or purpose in life. For some, this requires going through a full soul searching, having a profound mental and emotional cleansing in order to awaken and prepare us for the next level. If we can become aware and learn to listen for the proverbial call from our higher self/inner voice, then if we make the connection and trust our higher self when this occurs, we will become dialed in, doors will be opened for us to walk through, and our lives will improve and be so much smoother. Life's challenges are to awaken us so that we can grow, gain experience, and be all that we can be.

For some reason, we aren't taught to listen to ourselves; we're taught just the opposite. Take it from a guy who went through a lot of unnecessary suffering—start listening to your higher self. Take your power back. You'll be on track to overcome any challenge you face in your life. Even though intellectually I understood something was wrong with the way I mismanaged my thoughts, it took a while for me to wrap my mind around the fact of how powerful my thoughts were, how to harness them, and how to use them to benefit me instead of destroying me.

Learning to listen to my higher self changed my life dramatically. My higher self told me in no uncertain terms that Lynn was the woman I was meant to marry. That has been the greatest blessing in my life. I found my soul mate—the woman I will spend the rest of my life with. She's a wonderful wife and mother, and my life is complete with her and our children.

Though I don't buy into organized religion on a grand scale, there are some gems that come from all major religions that we can gather up and hold onto to help us on our way. One of my favorites comes from Buddhism: "If you suffer from poverty or illness for an extended period of time, it's a sign of ignorance." I realize now that for a long time I was ignorant of how powerful my thoughts were, that they do in fact create reality, and that I truly am a part of Source, a co-creator of my own reality. I have learned in other studies and in Quantum physics that people talk about creating reality by what they think, and how they focus their thoughts is what matters. They say, "The true reality is ..." and I can confirm from my experience that there is a truth to that.

We are interdimensional beings having an experience in this three-dimensional matrix called "reality." The true reality is that we can create any type of life we want for ourselves. Our thoughts affect everything in our lives. This is very well documented today. Just look at one book, *Messages from Water*, by Masaru Emoto. If thoughts can affect water crystals in the way the book explains, imagine what our thoughts are doing to us. We need to understand the formula in order to create the life we want. It's not as hard as you might think.

It's not a coincidence that you read this book. It was your intention. You manifested it. My entire purpose in writing this book was for you. Yes, *you*. My intention is that you may find something you can use to improve the quality of your life, that by reading about my experiences you'll find some assurance, courage, faith, and some tenacity, and that you can overcome any challenges you face, too. Take control of your thoughts. Keep them focused on what you want. Manage and focus your thoughts to create the life you want for yourself. If I can do it, I know with my entire heart that you can too. I assure you, you are perfect the way you are!

Know that you matter! Know you don't need to suffer! Know yourself! Know you are loved beyond imagination! By learning to know the consequences of your probable decisions, you gain perspective.

These are constructive, focused thoughts. You—just by feeling—know the difference between a constructive, focused thought and a destructive one. The result of the thought tells you. Having constructive, focused thoughts leads you to fulfillment; destructive thoughts lead to a place you've already been—anger, unhappiness, disappointment.

You want a coherent heart, a light heart. And a light heart comes by listening and expressing what it tells you, not by suppressing it.

To me the outcome was and is much deeper than having a wife and children in a comfortable permanent home. I was probably seeking it unconsciously my whole life. It took me so many years—a half century—to finally allow myself to be in a home with the ones I love and have no need to move anymore because I've found an important part within me.

Now I can take a deep breath and rest from hunting a ghost. I now know that being with Lynn and my children in a permanent home, having the space to think, comprehend, and feel peace and love is what I felt when I was on my grandfather's yacht. Of course, I thought that when I finally found that kind of peace in my own life, it would be on a real yacht. I didn't know I was simply seeking a home where I would feel loved and where I could express love. I had to sail through stormy, dangerous weather far out in the oceans by day and night, but I finally fulfilled my childhood dream.

I've found my yacht, and for now, it's safely docked at a beautiful island. I enjoy being here. I arrived with wounds and scars, but also with a treasure of all kinds of experiences.

But the most important part is that I brought the yacht home safe. Me!

There are so many different dreams out there, and no matter what, when, or where, everyone can get what they're dreaming of and create a life they love.

That includes you! You are the one you're waiting for. Believe in yourself! Always remember: I believe in you, no matter where you're coming from!

Our outer world is a reflection of our inner world.

Our inner world is a reflection of our thoughts.

Change your thoughts to change your world.

Authors like to finish their books with "The End." But I don't! I say:

THE BEGINNING

AFTERWORD

Thank you so much for reading my book. My hope is that it has helped to bring positive experiences into your life or the life of someone you know. If it has, please share them with me.

Send your experiences to Experiences@CrownRobert.com, or submit them privately through my website: CrownRobert.com

I look forward to reading them. Please indicate whether you want your message to be shared publicly through social media and, possibly, in an upcoming book.